T0207870

PHENOMENA

CODE OF THE

GRAND ORIGINAL DESIGN

Klaus Heinemann, Ph.D.

AND

Gundi Heinemann

BALBOA.PRESS

A DIVISION OF HAY HOUSE

Balboa Press books may be ordered through booksellers or by contacting:

Balboa Press
A Division of Hay House
1663 Liberty Drive
Bloomington, IN 47403
www.balboapress.com
1 (877) 407-4847

Print information available on the last page.

ISBN: 978-1-9822-3675-5 (sc)
ISBN: 978-1-9822-3677-9 (hc)
ISBN: 978-1-9822-3676-2 (e)

Library of Congress Control Number: 2019916141

Balboa Press rev. date: 10/14/2019

CONTENTS

Klaus Heinemann holds a doctoral degree in Applied Physics from the University of Tübingen, Germany. Dr. Heinemann looks back at a career in Materials Science and Surface Physics, including a Research Professorship at Stanford University, specialising in high-resolution electron optics. He also founded and led, until his retirement, a research corporation performing contract aero-thermodynamics research for NASA; and he co-founded a successful solar engineering corporation and holds patents for solar thermal collector design and ozone water treatment generators.

Gundi Heinemann is an educator by academic training, and an artist and a healing arts practitioner certified in numerous alternative healing modalities.

The Heinemanns are known for their pioneering research into the orb phenomenon. In 2007 Klaus co-authored the *"The Orb Project;"* and in 2010 Klaus and Gundi wrote *"Orbs, Their Mission and Messages of Hope."* Both titles were published world-wide in numerous languages. In 2013 they published *"Expanding Perception, Re-discovering the Grand Original Design,"* upon which this book builds.

Klaus and Gundi Heinemann served as keynote speakers on the orb phenomenon at several international conferences and were guests at over 50 radio and TV shows, including with Drs. Deepak Chopra, Miceal Ledwith, Norman Shealy, and William A Tiller. Klaus and Gundi's work on orbs was featured in Dr. Wayne Dyer's acclaimed book *"Wishes Fulfilled."*

1. INTRODUCTIONS

INTRODUCING THE AUTHOR OF THE FOREWORD

When we arrived on a Wednesday evening in 2002 at Emilia's[1] house for her weekly evening meeting, her living room was already filled to capacity with a group of people of Baha'i faith whom she had invited to her discussion group. It was our first exposure to people of Baha'i faith; and it was an utmost positive experience. There was an immediate kinship with every person in that group. They were sincere, open-minded, objective, unassuming, engaging, devout.

It would take another five years until our next experience with a person of Baha'i faith. This time it was a gentleman who was some 10-15 years senior to us. He exhibited, at the very onset of a relationship that would ensue and last ever since, the very same characteristics of human kindness, integrity and spirituality that we had experienced that evening in Emilia Rathbun's living room. This person was Dr. Stanislav Gergre O'Jack, the author of the Foreword of this book.

Stanislav O'Jack holds a Ph.D. in Clinical Psychology and has an educational and professional background in Mechanical Engineering, Architecture and Design, Industrial Design, and Education. During his long professional career, he was Headmaster of J. Krishnamurti's private school for children, tutored gifted children, worked in general

---

[1] Emilia Rathbun, co-founder with her husband Dr. Harry Rathbun of the Palo Alto, CA, based *Creative Initiative* and *Sequoia Seminar* Foundations, was a spiritual teacher to us ever since 1970, shortly after our immigration to the United States. After the passing of Harry in 1987, Emilia continued teaching and sharing her wisdom in seminars and weekly evening gatherings at her home in Palo Alto until her passing in 2004 at age 98. We introduce her in more detail in Appendix 3 of this book. See also our book titled *Being the change–how one contemporary person initiated extraordinary change in the world by following the wisdom teachings with totality.*

construction, and was employed in the space industry with a top-secret clearance. The project he had worked on made it to the 1969 moon-landing. Over decades, Dr. O'Jack worked with various mental testing procedures, pertaining to (1) dyslexia; (2) obsessive compulsion; (3) ADHD; (4) autism; (5) oppositional defiance; and in various Myer-Briggs assessments, from extrovert to introvert to ambivert.

In his foreword to *The Orb Project*,[2] Stanford University Professor Emeritus Dr. William A. Tiller included and described two "phenomenal" photos that had been taken through the solid black lens cap of the camera by his long-time friend, Dr. Stanislav O'Jack, who then initiated contact with us in this context. An intense exchange of communication with Stanislav about his "lens-capped" photography ensued, and two years later we spent a weekend with him and his wife Helen in Sea Ranch, California, where the four of us confirmed this photographic phenomenon. We describe a result of this weekend in Chapter 4.2 (*Non-Trivial Photographic Phenomena*).

We are honored that Dr. Stanislav O'Jack accepted our invitation to write a foreword to *Phenomena – Code of the Grand Original Design*. Indeed, Dr. O'Jack is no stranger to phenomena. In his foreword he describes some of his many personal phenomenological experiences. For who he is, a humble gentleman of Baha'i faith and a renowned scientist, the veracity of his words—as unusual as they may seem—is beyond reproach.[3]

---

[2] *The Orb Project*, by Miceal Ledwith and Klaus Heinemann, 2006.

[3] In our website "Phenomena," https://www.healingguidance.net/phenomena, we offer a blog with more personal phenomenological experiences of Dr. O'Jack.

FOREWORD BY DR. STANISLAV O'JACK

This latest book of Dr. Klaus Heinemann, co-authored with his wife and colleague, Gundi, a trained Energy Therapist, titled *Phenomena: Code of the Grand Original Design,* is for me a marvelous stimulus, as pertaining to the reality that there are still things science has yet to adequately codify.

Klaus, a physicist, shows an unusually strong, disciplined scientific orientation; and yet, simultaneously, he portrays an open mind in the midst of what can be deemed as an intellectual metamorphosis as related to the yet non-comprehensible element of "phenomena," which is well delineated in this book. His approach is in keeping with Neils Bohr's concept of "complementarity," such as, "If there is a comprehensive manner with which to study that which is labeled Science, then there must also be a comprehensive way with which to study the said-to-be 'Non-Science,' which includes phenomena, which are mystical occurrences referred to as originating from an unknowable source of infinite knowledge, also described with the use of the word GOD, aka "**G**rand-**O**riginal-**D**esign."

To support the theme of this new book, I will now relate to the reader several phenomenological events that have occurred in my own life. The first is an experience/episode of what I consider to have been an authentic event, one that I had with my late wife Jamal who died in my arms on March 12, 1991 from a lung-tumor. Jamal was a well-grounded person, a mental health social worker, a person who never believed in the paranormal, nor in UFOs, nor in the possibility of communication with those who have died and are in what is deemed the "afterlife."

One morning, circa 2006, at 6 am, as I sat on the edge of my bed while reciting prayers and contemplating what could be a positive outcome of a financial issue with which I had been struggling to resolve, I both felt and heard a tapping on the top of my balding head and the sound of my name "Stan" being uttered. I thought to myself, if HO'J (my present wife) has gone downstairs to prepare our breakfast, why is she now talking to me and why is she calling me "Stan" (as Jamal used to call me) instead of "Stanislav?" I looked to my right, and there was my deceased-wife, Jamal, sitting on the bed next to me, soothing my psyche by informing me that the money-issue will be taken care of successfully (which eventually it was). While we conversed, as guided by my educational background and training in Engineering and Psychology, and in my research in a paranormal physics project with physicist Dr. William Tiller regarding lens-capped photography, I consciously looked to see if I recognized her clothing attire, and if the bed was depressed where she sat. I did not recognize the clothing, but I could see that the bed was definitely depressed where she sat, and I could even see the bed-cover above the bottom-side of her body where she sat.

At that moment of contemplation as to my mental reality, I heard the click of the bedroom door behind me as the door opened, and in walked HO'J. I anxiously hollered and motioned to HO'J to quickly come to see Jamal. When HO'J arrived at my bedside, Jamal was gone. I then explained the latter to her, and she calmly replied, "How nice. Come downstairs, breakfast is ready."

Another strange but very real, personal experience I need to mention in this context is that I have successfully taken (sometimes experimentally/intentionally and at other times accidentally) a few hundred or more photographs with the lens of my camera securely capped, as seen/discussed in Klaus and Gundi's book *Orbs, Their Mission and Messages of Hope,* and as further mentioned in the chapter entitled *Non-Trivial Photographic Phenomena* in this book.

Yet another personally experienced episode has to do with some telephone calls that I received back on December 23, 2012, at about 2:30 pm. I answered an incoming call on the telephone and, amidst line-static, heard a voice say, "Hello Stanislav." I recognized the voice immediately, but still asked, "Who is it who is calling?" Then the voice said, "What do you mean when you say who is calling? It is me." The latter remark is how my personal close friend Vafa always identified himself in his telephone calls. Vafa had been dead for four years at the time of this telephone call. Vafa had called two days in a row during a heavy static noise condition. I looked at the caller ID on my answering machine, and what appeared was a series of "ones" and "zeros." I tried calling back to that number, but with no success.

Then, a few days later, I received another static noise telephone call. The voice said, "I was just passing by, so I thought I should say hello." The call was from another very close friend, Lesley. She had been dead for ten years. The same or a similar array of "ones" and "zeros" were on the caller ID. Once again, I attempted to call back for a longer telephone call conversation with her, but to no avail—the call on the ID did not go through.

In my numerous dream journals, many of my sightings of UFOs are recorded. The first one occurred in Ann Arbor, Michigan, in 1966, as I recall, when I drove home to visit my family. It was the same occurrence that was debunked by Dr. Hynek for the US Government. The next was in 1984, when I was within 100 feet of a UFO on the ground a few miles north of Laramie, Wyoming, at about 1 am. It was situated behind a six-foot high barbed wire fence, so I could not get closer to it. Just prior to that were two UFOs, about 1,000 feet overhead.

Then there were two sightings just north of Rock Springs, Wyoming, which I had encountered as I drove to my office in Jackson. In each case, I stopped my car, exited my car with camera in hand, so as to photograph them, and as I attempted to photograph the UFOs, in each instance, as I focused my camera to take a picture, it suddenly disappeared.

On a trip from Rock Springs to Cheyenne, Wyoming, at an altitude of about 7600 feet, I saw an air-born object to my right. My wife HO'J was driving and my mind was wandering. The noticed object was in a cloudless sky at approximately the same altitude as we were, but off in the distance, about five miles to the South. It was horizontal and flat in its shape, and traveling at the same speed as we were traveling. I thought to myself, how can an airplane travel so slowly? It was not a helicopter because of its configuration, and why at a speed such that it appeared to be tracking us? This went on for several minutes, and then, as I was looking at it, it vanished.

In my dreams, perhaps in an altered state, I have seen many flotillas of UFOs. In daylight, as I walk by/near gas street lights, they turn on or off regardless of the time of day. I can hold batteries in my hand to re-charge them, such as in this experience with MIT physicist Dr. Claude Swanson, who had traveled from Colorado to visit me at our home in Rock Springs, Wyoming, to discuss what he had heard regarding my personal experiences of taking photographs with a camera with its lens capped. We were viewing some of the photographs on a screen. To have an ease of discussing the photographs, I took out my laser pointer. It did not work. Dr. Swanson then grabbed it from my hand and tried to make it work. It did not. I then took the pointer, and I removed the batteries therein and held them between the palms of my hands. Dr. Swanson asked, "What are you doing?" I said that the batteries were cold and that I was warming them up, so they could/would work again.[4] He asked, with a load, piercing, unkindly voice, "How can someone with your educational background be so stupid?" Then, when the batteries warmed up, he tried the laser pointer again, and it worked. Dr. Swanson then said, "You have somehow just charged the batteries!"

The above information has been shared as a form of a preview, a preparation, a conditioning for the forthcoming eye-opening book *Phenomena – Code of the Grand Original Design*, which actually may be, or perhaps is, a Heinemann NASA-Consultant background expose in keeping with the current process of our own governmental

---

[4] Dr. O'Jack pointed out to me that, as a matter of course, he had made sure that the batteries had good electrical contact in their seat. They were positively depleted to the point that they did not work, before he re-charged them with his hands.

incremental increase in the release of utile Alien-oriented anciently-old information.

It is an honor and a blessing for me to have been asked to write a "foreword" for Klaus and Gundi's new book about Phenomena as Code of the "**Gr**and **O**riginal **D**esign," especially as concluded, proofed by myself, and sent on this very special day for me, on November 10th, 2018, which is the 200th anniversary of the birth-date, 1817, of the most recent Prophet of God: Baha-u-llah.

I now conclude my foreword,[5] and defer to Klaus and Gundi's new book *Phenomena – Code of the* **G***rand* **O***riginal* **D***esign.*

Stanislav O'Jack, Nov. 2018

---

[5] Dr. O'Jack provided much more information about his experiences with phenomena. We have included most of this additional material in a blog which we have been publishing in conjunction with the dedicated website of this book: "Phenomena," https://www.healingguidance.net/phenomena.

PREFACE

This book is a collaborative expression of a husband-and-wife team who have loved, valued and esteemed each other for over six decades. We, Adelgund ("Gundi") Roth and Klaus Heinemann, met when we were both still in high school and knew literally instantly that we would live our lives together. Among the many phenomena we are addressing in this book, the unfolding over many decades of this inner knowing is, arguably, among the most important and personal ones to mention.

Guidance from the "Realm of Unlimited Potential" is always available, to everybody and in every situation. But for some people it is not easy to detect. It is phenomenal, meaning it is not concrete, not factual, it can only manifest when we humans are ready to receive it.

We, Gundi and Klaus, were ready to detect that phenomenal "hint" at that early time in our lives, and what followed since that afternoon in July in Switzerland when we promised each other was just a continual falling in place—or a series of manifestations—of phenomenal occurrences: finishing our formal education, Gundi as teacher and Klaus as physicist, marriage, children, emigration from Germany and building new roots in the United States, finding and listening to new teachers, constantly being exposed to new phenomenal experiences, and finally becoming inspired to share what we have learned about the **G**rand **O**riginal **D**esign—the grandest phenomenon of all that is.

This is how we see it.

In general clarification of the pronouns we chose to use in the text of this book, Klaus wrote most of the analytical sections, and Gundi predominantly contributed the sections dealing with the personal, human factors as they relate to the healing phenomenon.

ABSTRACT

We are starting with what is usually considered a cardinal mistake for a common-interest book: presenting an abstract. It is customary for a scientific publication, but in a book one typically does not give away the "meat" upfront. Nevertheless, we think that, when presenting the synopsis of this book now, the reader may better understand the train of thought and be more at ease about skipping to any chapter of interest, while not losing the context for that chapter. Because an abstract is supposed to be short, its wording is necessarily a bit less colloquial—or sounding a bit more "scientific"—than in the main parts of the book. We apologize for this.

This book follows a calling I (KH) have had since my teens to contribute to bridging over the gap between science and spirituality. I later confined this task such that this bridge should not require (1) believing in channeling, (2) believing in reincarnation, and (3) considering the Bible as an infallible resource.

In preparation for the main part of the book, which deals with phenomena and their interpretation, we start with distinguishing between form and contents. They are an important duality. Both are important elements of the **G**rand **O**riginal **D**esign, which we introduce as a concept by pondering what we mean when we talk about GOD: "There is nothing that God is not, and there is nothing that is not God."

In a chapter on *Consciousness and Entropy* we then elaborate on my understanding as a physicist how we can leap to the plausible hypothesis of the existence of a dualism counterpart to the entire physical reality, which we call "spiritual reality." It is characterized by standard processing speeds being many orders of magnitude greater than the speed of light, and by absence of physical mass. We describe a hypothetical evolutionary process that starts in the spiritual realm and extends to the physical realm, and continues from there to the emergence of physical beings capable of reflective thought, who then "produce" consciousness through life experience. This consciousness is then re-deposited back in the spiritual realm, where it remains accessible indefinitely. According to this hypothesis, the functioning of this process is a major objective of the **Grand Original Design**. It portends that a human being is a vehicle to further evolve his creator.

To maximize the "production" of consciousness in a human lifetime, certain boundaries are set for the communication from the spiritual to the physical reality. They must assure that we humans are able to grow/evolve out of free will—certainly assisted by guidelines which we may perceive, but unimpeded by direct commands from there to us. We conclude that such communication, therefore, occurs via phenomena, which are unexplainable with current scientific understanding.

We describe that a new paradigm for scientific research is required if we want to make sense of phenomena.

Looking at a wide range of phenomena, from spirit orbs to crop circles to apparitions all the way to UFOs and ETs, we search for commonalities among them. The capability of intelligence on the other side of the veil to produce energies in the 10^{-16} Watt-second range, which is evidenced by the orb phenomenon, can plausibly be used for an explanation of all these other phenomena categories, and it can be used to rationalize the important phenomenon which we call spirit-directed healing.

Keeping in mind the self-evolving intent of the **Grand Original Design**, we argue that assisting in healing ranks very high on the list of priorities for highly intelligent beings in the nonphysical realm, and we presume that many of the phenomena we are seeing contain messages intended for us that are of the general nature of helping us and our environment and the planet to heal, or to stay healthy.

Examining in particular the UFO/ET phenomenon gives us clues about the relevance of Earth and Humanity within the **Grand Original**

Design. Making the bold assumption that no physical[6] being anywhere in the universe will ever be able to travel faster than at the speed of light, we conclude that no civilization anywhere in the universe—even though there are likely millions that exist concurrently with us—will ever be able to physically meet up with any other, or with humanity. Each one of this multitude of—presumably intelligent—civilizations in the Universe is, therefore, an independent evolutionary element of the **Grand Original Design**.

We briefly look at the hypothetical existence of parallel universes and conclude that this argument (of inability of physical UFO/ET-type contact with extraterrestrial civilizations due to speed of light limitations) may not be valid for civilizations that are based in a parallel universe. However, so little is known about parallel universes that we refrain from further speculation about this subject.

We conclude with remarks about the importance of human life in the scheme of the **Grand Original Design**.

An appendix is provided which is designed to contribute more depth about:

- The Energy→ Consciousness process;
- Consciousness as defined in the context of this book;
- Communication limitations between the realms; and
- Recommendations for Orb Photography.

---

[6] "Physical" is, in this context, defined as containing physical mass.

2. THE GRAND ORIGINAL DESIGN

A PHYSICIST EMBRACES PHENOMENA

The Grand Original Design provides that phenomena are meaningful for those who make room for them to occur in their world view, but that they can be discarded without direct, personal, detrimental consequences by those who choose not to give them credence.

I (KH) grew up in a lively fundamentalist Christian family environment. Until I left home for my university education, I was steeped into the belief system of born-again Christianity. This included exhaustive studies of the scriptures and the unquestioned acceptance of certain Christian belief elements. In my upbringing, the Bible would be the one and only authoritative document, upon which all interpretations of substance for life were—or had to be—based. I was involved in endless hours of reflection and debates on questions such as if wine and bread in the Holy Communion ritual are or represent the blood and flesh of Christ; or how Mother Mary could have been a virgin; how the world could have been created in seven days; how Jesus managed to feed a crowd of thousands with five loaves of bread and two fish; how Jesus's bodily resurrection could be rationalized; and so on. Each opinion in such discussions would be substantiated with Bible quotations. What made no sense was forged into a framework of understanding that was complicated and artificial, and mostly still did not make sense to my critical mind, no matter how long we labored over it.

Gundi's spiritual heritage was similar, except that she grew up in a more universal, open Christian setting. We both participated together in many of these discussions, focusing on topics how to maximize quality of life and contribute personally in a meaningful way.

After our immigration to the United States in our mid-twenties, a fundamental change in our approach to address questions about the meaning of life occurred. This process started just a few months after our arrival, when, while skiing in Squaw Valley, we met a German-American couple who were somehow different from the friendly but "superficial" Americans whom we had encountered up to that point in time. They introduced us to the work of Emilia and Dr. Harry Rathbun,[7] who lived in Palo Alto (actually just a stone's throw from the house we had rented at the time).

The Rathbuns headed a group that offered free evening courses which were called "The Challenge to Change" and "The Challenge of Time." We started frequenting meetings taught by their senior group members, held in private living-room group settings, and quickly became intrigued. New questions arose that became much more important for us. Who am I? What is the purpose of my life? Who— or what—is God? What is faith? Does God love non-Christians just as much as reborn Christians? How can I understand "Life" after life? Entertaining these and many more spiritually oriented questions would no longer occur by forging the arguments into a Bible-oriented framework. Using common sense became permissible.

Common sense does imply—and this is very important to express at the onset of this book—that there is room for the unexplained or unexplainable. As a physicist, I am used to discerning between that which can be explained—now or likely in the future—with the laws of physics, and that which is beyond such explanations. And indeed, there is plenty of the latter! In fact, it seems that the more we know and understand about reality, the more we realize how much we don't know.

---

[7] About forty years later, several years after they had passed, Gundi and I wrote a book (*Being the Change*, 2013) about aspects of the Rathbuns' teachings and our experiences with these remarkable people who, like none other among the many spiritual teachers we have personally known, realized every word of their teachings in their own lives.

For instance, the common understanding in physics used to be that the speed of light is the ultimate barrier—nothing can ever move faster. Now physicists are beginning to limit this understanding to what we call the "physical" reality, meaning that in the physical reality the speed of light is a real barrier,[8] while we open up the possibility of an entire additional reality that exists beyond the physical, in which normal velocities can be by many orders of magnitude faster than the speed of light. This additional reality—some call it the nonphysical reality, others "counterpart"[9] reality or even "spiritual" reality—resides beyond what is called our Minkowski space-time reality, i.e., it resides in the endless realm that extends beyond the speed of light.[10] It has no spatial and temporal boundaries. It is infinitely bigger than the physical reality. It is everywhere.

For me, common sense means that I cannot deny the existence of this immense nonphysical reality. I cannot deny that there is intelligence—likely even superb intelligence—in the nonphysical reality, and that this intelligence may at times try to exert a pointed influence on what is going on in the physical reality.

We will discuss later in this book that the **Grand Original Design**, according to which all that exists – the physical and nonphysical – is structured, demands that this influence is inherently of a "subtle" nature. For the law of increasing consciousness to work, this influence

---

[8] This statement has to be taken with a grain of salt. The jury is still out if, under certain circumstances, waves that do not contain physical mass can propagate at velocities a bit greater than the speed of light. One statement can, however, be made quite firmly: nothing that contains physical mass can move significantly faster than at the speed of light.

[9] *Expanding Perception* (2013).

[10] Some progressive physicists add this nonphysical realm to the physical reality and expand their understanding of the physical reality this way. They can then frame the entirety of the dual realities (physical and nonphysical) as one infinite reality. This "non-dualistic" view would be no different, other than describing the concept of a dualistic world view in nondual wording, attempting to demonstratively insist that there is only *one* reality.

cannot be direct or irrefutable but must remain in such a way that it cannot be scientifically proven.

This is then where phenomena come into play. It is, for me, perfectly plausible that intelligence from within the unseen, or nonphysical, reality tries to get our attention in our physical reality by means of what we call "phenomena." Phenomena are meaningful for those who make room for them to occur in their world view, but they can be discarded without direct, personal, detrimental consequences by those who choose not to give them credence. Much of this book deals with phenomena and their interpretation.

Getting back to the change of my personal world view, after internalizing the teachings of Harry and Emilia Rathbun many of the topics addressed in this book were, at one time or another, decades later, the subject of discussions with friends and family "from the past." But the course of such discussions would then be substantially different. I would no longer let myself get dragged into mental exercises about interpretations according to the scriptures. I am no longer interested in a biblical documentation of arguments. That is no longer of primary relevance to me. I am now interested solely in learning about what enriches life. Of course, much of this is unquestionably presented in the holy scriptures, but it no longer matters to me if it is or is not, at least not to the extent that such presentation would be considered of overreaching importance. After all, the biblical records date back almost 2000 years, and much has been learned by mankind during this long time.

A belief system is usually individualistic. No two people have exactly the same belief system. Mine reflects what is important to me, based on my personal experience and intuition. Yours will be different, at least in some aspects. It is not important who, or how many people, corroborate it, nor will I defer to a scripture quotation to make my point. The reader will know if what I say resonates, and he or she will usually be able to easily dig further into a subject matter of particular interest. In fact, the Internet is an ideal medium to accomplish this. Just google for specific key words, and you will quickly be presented with more information than you likely ever wanted to know about the subject matter at hand.

This book is a presentation of my personal world view, arrived at by research into the described subject areas to the point that it becomes persuasive to me. I do not intend it to be a scholarly work. I am not consistently following the traditional scientific approach of posing a hypothesis, researching literature on the aspects of the hypothesis, conducting new research, and presenting rational conclusions that sustain or refute the hypothesis. It is not my objective to present an exhaustive literary work with dozens of references underlining or refuting each statement I am presenting. I am not competing with other authors. I may at times simply make a statement, put it out there, and let the reader deal with it. It either speaks to him or her, or it doesn't.

I do, however, wish to address a premise which I consider quite important. To many spiritually oriented people the concept of channeling[11] is well known, and they have accepted the veracity of channeled information in their belief system. This occurs, however, often with limited discernment. It is my understanding that, even in the spiritual reality, where enormous wisdom is stored and in principle made available to any spirit entity incredibly fast, such wisdom must actively be researched (comparable to an Internet search), and different spiritual entities will have different opinions, experiences, preferences and interpretations.

Therefore, channeling must generally be taken with discernment, and the first question one should always ask when the topic of channeling comes up is, "Who is the entity that is channeling?" We have experienced over the years numerous highly intelligent

---

[11] In channeling a person's body or mind is (partially) being taken over by a spirit entity for the purpose of communication.

channeling entities, including *Abraham*,[12] *Theo*,[13] and many others. There are other famous Entities being channeled, such as *Ramatis*, the originator of several books on structures of the universe(s); *André Luiz* and *Emmanuel*, who channeled over 450 books through the famous Brazilian author Francisco ("Chico") Xavier;[14] and others.

Just as in real life, channeled wisdom is not always congruent. It must generally be understood as tailored to the audience. When taken out of context, it can be misleading or incorrect.

There is also the concept of reincarnation, which is an important element of major Eastern religions, including Buddhism and Hinduism. I am basing this entire book on the premise that the reader must not be presumed to believe in the veracity of the channeling process, or of any channeled material; nor is it a requirement that he/she holds reincarnation, or the verbal inspiration of the Bible as the Word of God, as a spiritual tenet. Instead, no religious belief system is required—all we ask for is openness with a minimum of prejudice.

---

[12] *Abraham* is portrayed to be a group of highly evolved spirit entities channeling wisdom through Esther Hicks.

[13] *Theo* is a group of twelve archangels channeling wisdom through Sheila Gillette.

[14] See Footnote 100.

FORM AND CONTENTS

Back in my high school years, I (KH) was known to be a good student in most academic subjects. But the subject "philosophy" never turned me on in those years. As I perceived it then, it was too vague, too verbose, too far removed from reality. But then, one day, our German literature teacher, who was an anthroposophist, made us reflect on the German poet and philosopher Friedrich Schiller's thinking about "form and contents," which he discussed in his *Aesthetical and Philosophical Essays*. It made a lot of sense to me to differentiate between these two terms. Form associates with beauty and aesthetics, but also with technique, how-to, and with pretense and superficiality. Contents, on the other hand, relates to essence, intent, depth, goodness, truth, realism.

I was always drawn to the contents part of the form-contents dualism. Over the ensuing decades, this distinction deepened and matured in my understanding. I strongly dislike superficiality, in every aspect of life, from artificial beautification with lipsticks and make-up of what I consider already naturally beautiful faces, to wearing clothing or exhibiting mannerism that is indicative of belonging to certain religious or elite groups.

A predominant emphasis on form, rather than content, is deeply entrenched in our Western society. Some of this is nice and desirable and fulfills a good purpose. The enjoyment of going to the symphony is definitely enhanced by wearing better than ordinary clothing. A religious service is uplifted by festive appearance of the clergy and the building in which it is held. I tend to more easily pick up a book in a bookstore if it has a pleasing cover. Beautiful architecture has its place. A website without attractive form will get less traffic than a site that is only content-driven. No question about that. But I react negatively when form becomes an obsession. What must I wear, how must I move, what must I say to be accepted as part of the clan? I'd rather not want to be part of it if it means that I must conform in a certain way. I guess we all know situations like this.

When it comes to religion, or religions, the wide-spread misunderstanding between form and contents stands out everywhere you look. Jesus teaches to give alms without making a big deal about it. But who does so? We are to pray in modesty with sincerity, to let it be a way of life rather than a string of words; yet great effort is made everywhere to come up with the most refined, often eloquent, impressive language to formulate our prayers. What's the purpose of expensive churches, cathedrals, mosques, temples, synagogues? Wouldn't a more modest place of gathering often be more appropriate to get in touch with our essence, or with God?

One of the most important places of Christianity is the St. Peter's Basilica in Rome. I have had the privilege of visiting there many times over several decades. The sensation of being in that majestic cathedral has, to me, never been one of spirituality, sacredness, calmness, love, peace, being in the presence of God. To this day, the best words to describe the feeling I am having when visiting this "church of all churches" is grandiose, overwhelming, spectacular, intimidating. It never impressed me as a particularly religious or sacred place where I would find infilling for my soul. For that to happen, I would look for a place much more modest, yet imbued with spirituality, such as the church of the *Community of Taizé* in central France, or the little nondenominational chapel in Sea Ranch, California.

I see the distinction between form and contents as particularly vital in the field of alternative healing, specifically when it comes to spirit-directed healing. Common to essentially all the modalities Gundi and I have studied and practiced over the years is that everybody is said to be able to learn and apply the modality. But what does the learning entail? Are we saying that everybody can learn the technique of the modality, or is it that everybody can become a healer? Is there a difference between the two? What would it be? If we were really clear about this distinction, the numerous alternative healing modalities offered all over the globe would be taught very differently, indeed!

Let's look at Reiki, which is arguably the most commonly practiced of all alternative healing modalities. There is hardly any person calling him- or herself a healing arts practitioner who is not a Reiki Master or, at minimum a Reiki level 1 or 2 practitioner. Every one of them knows that Reiki has two components: hand positions and symbols. Some teachers emphasize correctness of the hand positions. Others are adamant about the correct drawing and application of the symbols. But is that really what healing is all about? Does it really matter how precisely I place my hands, how nice or how accurately I draw the symbols? Does that affect the healing of my client? Or is it my intention behind these formalities that really matters? Am I not simply the conduit for Reiki healing to occur? Is it not my state of mind, the love and compassion I am radiating toward the client, is it not the bridge I help building between the client and the "Realm of Infinite Potential" that matters?

We have taken Reiki just as an example. One can select any other spiritual healing modality and ask the same questions. Hand positions have a major importance in many modalities, such as Quantum-Touch, Jin Shin Yuitsu, Healing Touch, Pranic Healing, to name just a few of those which we have studied and practiced. Other modalities focus on correctly verbalizing intentions, on a correct form of prayer or meditation—on fulfilling certain requirements that are, ultimately, nothing but formalities.

One side never fully describes a situation. And so it is with this brief discussion of form and contents. In nature, the two are often perfectly blended. Look at a beautiful flower. The just-perfect blend of shape, color, and fragrance of a rose make up its beauty. Where does form end and content start? One does not end, and the other does not start; together they make up the essence of a rose. Take music. One could say it's all content and no form, but is that really so? A friend gifted me the construction plans to build a very high-quality loudspeaker system.[15] What a world of difference there is between listening to my favorite symphonic music through such a perfect sound system, compared to the speakers of my laptop or even the not-at-all shabby stereo system my friend's design had replaced! The same concerto! Clearly, the content is the same either way, but the addition of perfect form—in this case a perfect sound system—dramatically elevates the experience.

We have written much about that this physical world is a world of dualisms. Form and contents constitute such a dualism. In this sense, they are an integral part of our life experience. Contents is related to the essence, the soul, that which is not subject to space-time limitations and will not decay. Form, on the other hand, is related to beauty, to the feeling, sensing aspect of life. It does not have eternal connotations, but it certainly "seasons" the wonderful moments life presents.

We know that following certain forms, or formalities, will actually help prepare us for the inner attitude that is what matters when it comes to healing. Form helps us get closer to the essence, but form is not essence in and by itself. To provide a nice atmosphere in the alternative healing arts office is tremendously helpful for the overall experience of the client. Tasteful decorations, warm colors and lighting, perhaps calming music, positively contribute to the healing experience. Gundi has always been meticulous with making her healing practice studio look nice, welcoming, uplifting. You step in and feel engulfed by beauty. It's not the size of the room that matters, not the dollars spent on decoration, but the taste of execution: the color schemes chosen; the warmth of the fabric on the treatment table and the crystal bed; the wall coverings, choice of pictures, choice of lighting, and the crystals and books exhibited. All this is

---

[15] The late Siegfried Linkwitz, proprietor of Linkwitz Labs and scientific mastermind and developer of high-end speaker systems, gifted me the plans for building this speaker system. According to his superbly detailed plans, where the placement of each component—down to the detail of a screw—and millimeter accuracy contribute to the just perfect end result, I put together a sound system that makes all the world of a difference for the listening pleasure of a favorite piece of music.

form, but it helps prepare the client to receive that which matters, which is the content of the treatment. It's like the calcium we need in our nutrition: eating it with spoons will not do it—very little of it will then be absorbed by the body; but, instead, taking it in the correct form, the correct proportions, and correct combination with other nutrients is important for proper absorption.

An understanding of the difference between form and contents will greatly help us understand much of what life, death, immortality, fame, and soul are really all about. The more we ponder these distinctions, the closer we will get to the meaning of our own life here on earth.

THE GRAND ORIGINAL DESIGNER

... there is nothing that God is not, and there is nothing that is not God ...

Back in the 1990s I spent much time philosophizing with a friend about esoteric topics. Ben had spent a professional lifetime in organization management consulting and was an adamant believer in contextualizing spiritual expressions. We would spend hours on end "framing," i.e., trying to define who or what "God" is or entails. Framing the concept of GOD as the perfectly descriptive and fitting English-language acronym for "**G**rand **O**riginal **D**esign," as we first did in our book *Expanding Perception*, had not yet been intuited at the time when Ben and I had these discussions, even though our conceptual understanding of this description was clearly on the mark.

It helps to approach the objective of understanding what God is when we try to express what God is not. For example, most people would undoubtedly agree that God is not a wise, male, predominantly judging, human-like figure residing somewhere in the skies, even though this is precisely the image that has prevailed in many cultures for millennia—it is what is still widely portrayed in church services and in religious scriptures (the Old Testament, and also widely in the New Testament, and in sacred scriptures of various not Judeo-Christian religions).

This unfortunate description of God having noble human characteristics is also the most prevalent underlying reason for atheism today. People who allow themselves to apply some common sense to traditional religious interpretations simply come to the point of calling much of this "nonsensical." That kind of God-figure is below their intellectual level of tolerance, and they outright reject it and call themselves atheists. They do not realize that they are rejecting an outdated understanding that is, indeed, worthy of being replaced with a more solid, more contemporaneous world view.

The simple circumstance that it is still difficult for me to overcome my conditioned habit of addressing God in the masculine tense (the "He" form) underlines this wide-spread misconception.[16] God is more than that. God has no gender. God is not a human-like being. God is not a nebulous entity that desires to be believed in, and that judges people depending on how much they adore and praise It.

God is also more than "things" and more than "energy," which is the "mother" of things. God is also Thought and Consciousness. God is the Consciousness from which all things and all thought originate and continue to develop.

The human mind has created a mathematical scale that extends from minus infinity ($-\infty$) to plus infinity ($+\infty$). Conventional thinking considers values on this scale and defines as evil values on the negative side, and as good that which is on the positive side. This is an unfortunate and often misleading valuation system. God is not confined to the positive side of the scale. God is on the entire scale! God is everything: that which we call good and that which we, in our limited human wisdom, call evil. It would be much more appropriate to think in terms of letting the value scale start at zero, not at minus infinity. Then we can easier understand that what is near zero is perhaps small, insignificant, undeveloped, unevolved, primitive, ignorant, unconscious, but not evil.

No change in human thinking would be more beneficial for the ever-evolving **Grand Original Design** than doing that which facilitates climbing upwards on this scale, working on that which "educates," which "leads out of" the lower degree on the scale of consciousness, which is ignorance. That, of course, is the original meaning of the word education (rooted in Lat. *educare*—to train, mold, form, as well as Lat. *educere*—to lead out).

---

[16] I was conditioned to pray to God by addressing "Him" as "Father," as I would address a distinguished person. There is certainly nothing objectionable about this, in particular since the new understanding is not at odds with this sort of personalized understanding of what God is: it is certainly inclusive of any imaginary personification. But God is much more than any such a human construct.

God is more than thought and consciousness. It includes the "Spirit" which prompted the **G**rand **O**riginal **D**esign with all its potentiality to unfold. The creative action of that spirit is not a matter of the past but is timeless. It is ongoing at every moment and at every point within the Universe. It has the unlimited potentiality to introduce change of every magnitude at any point in the physical universe, including in our individual lives—in matters which we call health and healing.

Most religions agree: God loves indiscriminately, the ignorant and the knowledgeable, the weak and the strong, the evil and the good. Our late teacher Dr. Harry Rathbun used to re-phrase this statement this way: "The Universe is benevolent toward the development of consciousness." But God is more than an "entity" that loves. God is more than a Christian, a Jewish, Arab, Hindu, Buddhist, Taoist, more than any and all belief systems. God is more than the Creator. God is not confined to a gender. God is more than a physical entity of any kind. God is beyond space and time.

God is more than any of these, because each of these terms is defining, and God is not definable. Whenever we try to define what God is, we have already missed it. God is more, always more. God does not fit into any frame. Because, there is always an outside with regard to a frame, and God is, in addition to what is inside the frame, always also all that which is outside. All we can say is, "God is; there is nothing that is not God, and there is nothing that God is not—God is everything: every thing and every no-thing."

Native Americans use the term "Creator." That word is much more descriptive, fitting and less controversial. But even the word Creator is defining. Out of what has God created? Is that original substance from which all was created not also God? If it were not, then there would be room for other creations that would not be God, and that would be contradictory to the understanding that there is nothing that God is not, and there is nothing that is not God.

Modern natural sciences, in particular physics and astronomy, are well ahead of the religious sciences when it comes to the new understanding of what God is. Without making any statement of belief or spirituality, and hence truly outside of religious confines, many modern physicists and astronomers agree that the original substance, or energy, from which everything originates that is and ever will be or may ever evolve into, is undefined and undefinable, hence "mysterious." It will never be comprehensible. And, thus, we may find that a good expression of the essence of God is "Mystery."

That Mystery, from which everything originates, contains unlimited potential to unfold:

- into endless numbers of universes, among which our universe is one;
- into somewhere around 100 billion galaxies in our universe, among which our Milky Way is one;
- into several hundred billion planets in our galaxy, and probably in every one of these billions of other galaxies, many of which can evolve and sustain conscious life, such as our earth;[17]
- and into life, such as on earth, that can produce consciousness, wisdom and love.

On the basis of this insight of modern natural sciences we can therefore state that "God is evolving itself."[18] It is like a learning computer. It is like a comprehensive computer program that learns from the engagement of users with it. Every time a user employs the program to solve a problem, the program incorporates the learnings

---

[17] It is not necessary to assume that all these planets sustain life concomitantly. Given the truly incomprehensibly long physical time that has elapsed since the "Big Bang" started our universe some 13.5 Billion years ago, the probability that another planet with life similar to human life at our current stage of evolution existed at any time in the history of the Universe, is approximately 100 million times higher than the probability that such a planet exists concurrently with our lifetime. (If we define a "human lifetime" arbitrarily as 130 years, then 100 million such "lifetimes" fit into the 13 Billion-year history of our universe). See much more on this in Chapter 4.3.

[18] This characteristic of GOD is distinguishing from what is known as pantheism.

from that engagement into itself and, from that moment on, makes it readily available to others who might also be looking into a similar problem.

Looking closer at our acronym formulation, we must find that even the words "Grand Original Design" are insufficient to get a hold of what God is. It would be more fitting to replace the word "Design" with the active words "Designer of Everything." If we then tweak the definition of the word "Designer" to include, in this context, everything that has ever been designed, all the products, features, variances, and design potentialities, we may be getting close to what God is: "The **Grand Original Designer,** the maker of every thing and every no-thing that is, ever was, and ever will be."

Let us engage in a thought experiment. If this were true, how would that which created everything communicate with us? Would this communication only be through facts that we can understand, comprehend, calculate?

3. CONSCIOUSNESS AND ENTROPY

The Grand Original Design included, in its manifestation of the physical universe, a mechanism to evolve ever-increasing consciousness. GOD is evolving itself, and you and I are vehicles for this to happen. The relevant question is then, "How much consciousness is each one of us contributing in our lifetimes?"

UNIVERSAL CREDO

I believe in the creative, unitive power of the Cosmos:

Energy
Light
Love
Oneness.

From this Oneness all that is has come to be:

One Source of all that exists,
One Direction of Evolution
Toward complexity and Consciousness,
One Intelligence, permeating everything,
One Will, holding in implicate order
The answers to all questions asked,
One Love, drawing all who are open
To creativity, wisdom, and wholeness.

We and all space are one,
We and all time are one,
We and all life are one.
We share One Earth,
We are One Humanity,
We are to be One Spirit.

I invoke the creative unitive power of the Cosmos
To express through me,
To work through me,
To manifest through me
Truth, Beauty, and Goodness

Emilia Rathbun (1906 - 2004) wrote and dedicated this poem as Introduction to Klaus Heinemann's 1991 book *"Consciousness or Entropy?"*

THE UNIVERSE IS BENEVOLENT

"The Universe is benevolent toward the evolution of consciousness."

Harry Rathbun

"The Universe is providing; life's purpose is expansion of consciousness." Pierre Teilhard de Chardin believed so; and it was, as we said earlier, one of the favorite statements of Stanford University Law Professor Dr. Harry Rathbun (1894 - 1987), who became a spiritual teacher to us shortly after we immigrated to the United States in 1969.

Harry would elaborate on this important statement during his famous annual commencement addresses which he gave at Stanford, and which graduates and faculty members alike would not want to miss. Together with his wife, Emilia Rathbun, Harry taught numerous seminars at the Sequoia Seminar grounds in Ben Lomond, California, which we started to attend in 1970. The seminars would typically end with a lecture by Harry, where he would explain the statement in more depth. The universe is not just the product of a random cataclysmic event that happened some 13.5 billion years ago, which then, in a succession of countless random evolutionary developments ended up where we are now. Instead, he argued that what happened at that "point zero" of space and time was based on an unfathomable amount of thought and intention which included clear directionality, a blueprint for the evolution of everything that would follow. That evolution had one specific goal: the expansion of consciousness. Much of what we present in this book focuses on this topic.

"The Universe is benevolent toward the evolution of consciousness." For quite some time I have felt the nudge to share some thoughts why I feel so strongly about this statement. Do I really, deep down in my belief system, accept this enormous wisdom as truth? Do I trust in a positive outcome? Is goodness prevailing?

As I look back over the recent decades of my life, I feel a sense of immense gratitude about having been shown, over and over again, that the Realm of Unlimited Potential has nothing but the very best in store for mankind. There is overwhelming evidence that great, powerful, individual and collective consciousness exists beyond the veil of the physical reality. "They" strive to demonstrate to us that They want to help us on all levels of our being, so we can maximize what we came to experience in this physical lifetime.[19] Nothing but love, pure, unconditional agape, is beaming toward us from that dimension.

But then, this is easy to say for me, a member of a small minority of comparatively privileged people in this world—simply by virtue of living in a place where abundance and beauty, law and order, and liberty and freedom of expression prevail. But what about the others? What about those who lost their homes or livelihood in the floods, droughts, earthquakes, hurricanes, typhoons that seem to hit this earth more and more frequently? What about the millions of refugees from war-torn countries, what about the unfortunate fellow human citizens who are persecuted for the color of their skin or the way they pray, or who cannot earn enough to feed their family, and who are trying to find a new basis for life elsewhere, in a country where nobody wants them? How can the loving universe tolerate such injustices?

Many people have long accepted and deeply believe and trust in the "Grand Original Design." For them, a 12-oz glass with 6 oz of water in it is half-full. The universe is benevolent toward the evolution of

---

[19] With this phrasing, we do not mean to communicate that reincarnation is a necessary part of the Grand Original Design. While I am personally persuaded that reincarnation is an entirely plausible concept, belief in it is not a stringent requirement for, or a conclusion of, the hypotheses presented in this book. More generally, our conclusions are meant to be neutral to belief systems of any kind of religion.

consciousness! Is it? "Of course," they say, "how else could life and the beauty around us have come about?" They have no problem believing in a universal law stating that consciousness is ever-accumulating. For them it is self-evident that crop circles, apparitions, near death experiences, out-of-body experiences, orbs, and other phenomena that may even include UFOs are not man-made or coincidental physical happenings, but rather manifestations from a realm beyond the physical. They believe that our physical well-being is always divinely orchestrated. They are convinced that mending a broken relationship is a process that involves Spirit Entities, invisible to our physical eyes, that are always around us and that are intent on helping us in whichever way they can. They value intuition and listen to it. And they know that Existence is multi-facetted, that the physical realm is only a small fraction of Reality at large, and that their own life is not limited by the 4-dimensional space-time physical reality but extends well beyond into other types of dimensions.

When reading this book, we hope that these people will find themselves reinforced in their beliefs. But for the vast majority of the seven billion co-inhabitants of this world, these conclusions are not self-evident. They have trouble with them. For many of them the proverbial glass is half-empty, not half full. The thinking we find natural is everything but natural for them. They reject everything that they assume cannot be explained with what our scientists have discovered.

It is primarily these people whom we are targeting with this book. I boldly state that their world view is based on unawareness that the scientific discoveries they cling to are limited by an antiquated, outdated, obsolete scientific paradigm.

Let us continue with our thought experiment: If it were true that the Universe is benevolent toward the evolution of consciousness, how would that which created everything communicate this circumstance to us? Would this communication only be through facts that we can understand, comprehend, calculate? What other kind of communication would "They" use?

Phenomenological experiences give credence to the existence of a nonphysical reality, or spiritual reality. Since the only "realistic" way of direct communication from the nonphysical to the physical reality is via phenomena, i.e., via effects that are not scientifically verifiable, the irrefutable occurrence of phenomenological experiences in our lives corroborates the supreme cognitive character of the spiritual reality.

Back in the winter of 1979, I spent an entire family skiing vacation with what in retrospect I can best describe as "automatic writing," on the subject of dualism realities. We had rented a modest cabin near Lake Tahoe and looked forward to a week of skiing with our 11 and 13-year old sons. It turned out different. Gundi did go skiing with the kids, and I started and kept writing literally day and night—in longhand; the age of the computer had not yet arrived at the Heinemann family.

The resulting manuscript, which I titled *Consciousness or Entropy?* consisted of four main sections.[20]

- ■ The first part dealt with the hypothesis that the entire physical reality—earth, solar system, Milky Way galaxy, and the billions of more distant galaxies—could be understood as just one dualism aspect of an all-encompassing "Supreme-Original Reality." Initially I called the other dualism reality aspect simply "counterpart reality" and later identified it as having all typical characteristics of what people would commonly understand as "spiritual reality." The two dualism realities would be analogous to the "particle"/"wave" dualism in physics. Energy and thought, and entropy[21] and

---

[20] We have added a more explicit summary of the *Consciousness or Entropy?* manuscript in Appendix (A) of this book.

[21] In physics, entropy is defined as used, no longer usable physical energy.

consciousness, are critical dualism elements in the spiritual reality.

- The second part of the manuscript discusses that the **Grand Original Design** provides that consciousness is the end-product of a two-step "creative process" that involves the physical universe to be realized: first step was the creation of the physical and spiritual universes from supreme-original energy in what is commonly called the "Big Bang." The second used the potential that is embedded in that act of creation, for intelligent life to evolve to the point that consciousness (wisdom), the intended outcome, can be "produced" and cosmic consciousness can thus be continually enhanced. This means that the **Grand Original Design** included its own evolution to ever-increasing cosmic consciousness. GOD is evolving itself, and, on planet earth, the human is a vehicle for this to happen.[22]

- Part three of *Consciousness or Entropy?* looks at energetics. This entire process consumed an enormous amount of physical energy until it started to produce this intended outcome. Consumed physical energy is called "entropy." Hence, we have a process of increasing complexity and of increasing consciousness as duals of what we can call the Supreme Creation Process. The question is for each one of us humans who are privileged to live in this time and place, "How much consciousness are we generating and contributing to cosmic consciousness as a byproduct of the unavoidable amount of entropy—wasted energy—which we are accumulating as we are living our lives?"

- Finally, in part four, we look at communication between the dualism realities. The speed of light is the barrier, or the veil, between the two—physical and spiritual—realities.

---

[22] For more about this see the chapter "The Law of Increasing Consciousness" and Appendix (A).

Processes in the physical reality are limited to velocities less than the speed of light; and in the spiritual reality they are predominantly many orders of magnitude faster than the speed of light. The **Grand Original Design** ingeniously provides impediments for crossing this barrier in either direction. Transitioning from the physical to the spiritual reality is practically prohibited by this law of physics, which is applicable for anything that contains physical mass (or matter). However, human thought is not subject to this restriction.[23] With thought capacity, the human freely penetrates into – and functions inside of – the spiritual realm. Transitioning from the spiritual to the physical reality is also possible, but since the former does not contain any mass or matter, the effect of crossing this veil is not easily perceived or materially manifested in the physical reality. Such manifestations do occur under certain circumstances, but their appearances are subject to uncertainty and unpredictability, similar to the uncertainty principle in quantum physics. Their interpretation is not determinative. This is arguably the most ingenious aspect of the **Grand Original Design**.

The ramifications of the communication restraints between the physical and spiritual realities are awesome and are emphasized in later chapters in this book. In particular, the limitation of velocities in the physical reality to, at maximum, the speed of light reduces to essentially zero the probability that any two intelligent physical civilizations in the physical universe will ever be able to meet and communicate directly, face-to-face with each other[24]. Unrealistically

---

[23] More about this is presented in Appendix (A).

[24] Please understand that, here and in all other places in this book where we talk about physical encounters between physical beings, we pragmatically and exclusively refer to just that, physical encounters, which we define as including physical structures (vehicles) and physical bodies containing the nonphysical aspects of intelligent beings, similar to the physical human body "containing" the nonphysical human soul. Any sort of telepathic communication is outside of this definition.

long physical travel times and other severe physical and biological constraints dictate this conclusion. We are, in a subsequent chapter, emphasizing that the laws of physics render any argumentation impossible that biological beings could ever travel faster than at the speed of light. Considering the distances in the universe, this means that we are alone and independent with regard to our human challenge to fulfill our destiny by becoming wiser, more conscious, more loving beings during our lifetimes.

Continuing with the thought experiment, since direct physical communication between humanity and intelligent life forms on other planets can be ruled out, and since, on the other hand—as we discuss in the next chapters—we are ubiquitously being contacted from somewhere in ways which cannot be explained scientifically, it appears that phenomenological contact experiences in and by themselves give credence to the existence of what we called the dualism counterpart reality, or spiritual, reality.

Furthermore, since the only "realistic" way of direct communication from the nonphysical to the physical reality is via phenomena, i.e., via effects that are not scientifically verifiable, the irrefutable occurrence of multi-facetted phenomenological experiences in our lives corroborates the supreme cognitive character of the spiritual reality.

When I, reluctantly and insecure,[25] shared the draft of that writing with Harry and Emilia, they were exceedingly affirmative and encouraging and spontaneously invited me to present the material to a large group of their seminarians.[26]

---

[25] I was very concerned about the theologically "radical" character of these writings and conclusions.

[26] The presentation took place in the spring of 1980 in the "Las Alas" meeting hall of Sequoia Seminar in Ben Lomond, California, to a group of about 100 people, who overwhelmingly encouraged me to further pursue these thoughts.

It took several more years until, in 1991, I had the courage to publish this material, which at the time I considered to be very controversial,[27] as a book, entitled *Consciousness or Entropy?* Emilia Rathbun wrote the "Universal Credo," with which this Chapter was prefaced, as introduction to that book.

---

[27] I was primarily concerned about not wanting to offend fundamentalist Christians, whom I esteem as my spiritual heritage.

TIME

"Your time is limited, so don't waste it by living someone else's life."
Steve Jobs

Time is defined as "the period between two events during which something exists, happens, or acts."[28] Our time—in this lifetime—is precious. Time is all we got. But do we really treat time as a most precious asset?

As a child and during my adolescence, I (KH) did not think of time that way at all. When I was five, I would count the minutes when my time of a prescribed nap was up and I could go outside and play. When I was in school, I would count the years until, finally, I would have my schooling behind me and "real" life could begin. In fact, to this day, waiting has never been my strong side, regardless of the situation in which I find myself needing to be patient. I sometimes wonder how much time, in aggregate during my life so far, I have spent devising ways or mechanisms to prevent having to wait.

I chose the topic of my academic studies, physics, over what I otherwise would have preferred at the time to have studied, medicine, because of half a year of "waiting" for the start of medical school, while enrolling in physics was immediately open to me after finishing high school. I finished grad school with the diploma in physics in the minimum time requirement (4 years after high school), because I did not want to "waste" time with extracurricular activities, such as fraternities, collegial sports, and alike. And I started my Ph.D. thesis immediately after grad school and completed my degree in record two years.

Later, after we had immigrated to the United States, selecting the house where we ended up living since 1971 was, to a good extent, based on the ease of getting to destinations from there, such as to

---

[28] *Your Dictionary.com.*

NASA, where I worked at the time, and to the freeways to get to places. The beauty factor of that choice—very important to Gundi—came second for me.

I hate spending time shopping—in and out is my *modus operandi*. If I find something I like, I buy two, or three, or a bunch of it, so I won't have to "waste time" shopping there that soon again.

The list goes on and on. Even later in life, when I considered myself more mature and insightful, I would still adhere to my "time conserving" habit. On our many road travels, I generally plan routes and travel times to avoid rush hour congestions, and, more recently, I would always be aware of yellow or red lines appearing next to our route of travel in the navigation device built into the dash board of my car, indicating traffic slowdowns. In fact, on our long road travels—we would rather drive and be entertained by good radio broadcasts or CDs than wait in airports—I would let my navigation device tell me when we would likely arrive and then try to adjust our gas and food stops such that we would make that originally predicted arrival exactly on time.

Time is our birthright. It's what has been given to us. What we do with it is what matters. As a physicist, I am aware of the second law of thermodynamics, or the "law of entropy." As time goes by, we expend physical energy—always, without exception—and that energy is never recoverable. It is lost for good. Gone. Dissipated in the form of no further usable thermal energy, or heat, every so little increasing the temperature of everything. The all-important questions for us to pose are then, "What is there on the other side of the law of ever-increasing entropy? Is there something that is of lasting benefit? What is it that makes the expense of time worth the while?"

The latest edition of the key contents of the aforementioned book *Consciousness or Entropy?* was published another 22 years later, in 2013, under the carefully selected title *Expanding Perception, Re-Discovering the Grand Original Design*. This title could hardly be more descriptive of the contents of the book, as revised: "What life is all about is expanding our perception by continually enlarging the circles of our attention, so that we may more live by the purpose and intent of the **Grand Original Design**." This, as we discuss in further details in the next chapter, is to be a vehicle for ever-increasing cosmic consciousness. The challenge for us is to recognize that this entails, first and foremost, that we become loving, compassionate human beings.

For this to occur, within the short time given to us in this incarnation, it will greatly help if we open up to the way with which the Conscious Potentiality on the other side of the veil, which very much desires us to succeed and wishes to help us on our way, communicates to us: via phenomena.

THE LAW OF INCREASING CONSCIOUSNESS

"We may, perhaps, imagine that the Creation was finished long ago. But that would be quite wrong. It continues still more magnificently, and at the highest levels of the world." **Pierre Teilhard de Chardin**

Every action, or even thought, comes at the expense of a finite amount of physical energy that is converted to entropy; and there is concomitantly the inherent potential of "creating" – ever so much or little – consciousness as a "by-product." The question for each one of us human beings who are privileged to live in this time and place, is then, "How much consciousness are we generating and contributing to cosmic consciousness as a byproduct of the unavoidable amount of entropy – wasted energy – which we are piling up as we are living our lives?"

Form and content relate like *awareness and consciousness*. If there is one thing we have come to be sure about, it is that life has a purpose, and the purpose is connected to "consciousness." Consciousness is more than awareness. It is awareness in context. We are not conscious if we can recite the "Our Father," but we grow in consciousness if we apply in our life what this profound prayer states. We are not conscious when we have learned the names of hundreds of plants in our garden, but we have made a leap in consciousness when we treat the nature around us as a gift given to us and others to enjoy.

In *Expanding Perception, Re-Discovering the Grand Original Design*, the gift of intuition was given to us to write about the "Law of Increasing Consciousness."[29] It states that every physical action of

---

[29] As we have described in *Expanding Perception*, consciousness is the end-product of a two-step "creative process" that involves the physical universe. See also Appendix (A). The first step is what we commonly describe as the "Big Bang," the singular event that occurred some 13.5 billion years ago when a huge quantum of cosmic energy was converted into physical energy—and hence physical mass, which is a state of physical energy. That conversion process included the potential

a human being, which invariably leads to an increase of entropy—i.e., not further usable energy—has the potential of an increase in consciousness as by-product. Entropy and consciousness go hand in hand, and it is our challenge to maximize consciousness in this "energy → consciousness" human life process.[30]

While we have described the Law of Increasing Consciousness in detail in our *Expanding Perception* book, we are invariably faced with this set of questions which are often asked but seldom addressed:

- Why is it that, given this noble intent in the creation of the universe, so much suffering exists in the world?
- Why hasn't all this consciousness that has already been "produced" over the centuries, even millennia, made this world truly a better place?
- Why are billions—not millions, but billions—of fellow citizens of this great planet, with all its wonderful potential, living under terribly impoverished conditions?
- Why are there hunger, disease, catastrophes?
- Why are there such huge differences between the "haves" and the "have nots" in this world, such as Gundi and I have, for example, witnessed on our travels to the *Oneness University* in Southern India or to other places in the Third World?

---

for biological matter to emerge on Earth, culminating in human life—and probably on many other earth-like planets elsewhere in our galaxy and beyond. The second creative step is that this biological creation, has become so powerful, through the evolution of man/woman, i.e., "creatures" with reflective thought capacity, that it has the potential to apply thought and experiences to "create" consciousness, which is the intended outcome. This outcome, as designed, can preferably be achieved in this dual-step process that involves physical/biological beings in the physical universe. The Grand Original Design, with which the Big Bang was empowered, included all this potentiality for the creation of consciousness. It included its own evolution to ever-increasing cosmic consciousness. GOD is evolving itself, and man is a vehicle for this to happen.

[30] These thoughts follow the teachings of the French philosopher and Jesuit Priest Pierre Teilhard de Chardin (1881 – 1955), who, in his posthumously published book "*The Phenomenon of Man*," described an ever-increasing evolutionary process of complexity and consciousness.

- Why have we been killing each other, with more and more cruel weaponry?
- Why do we continue to live at the brink of self-destruction? Are we not all humans, do we not all belong to the one human family?
- Why has all this "consciousness" not turned this planet into a paradise? If the universe is truly benevolent toward the evolution of consciousness, why can we not live in freedom and peace with each other?

These are troubling questions, and much has been written world-wide and throughout the centuries, in an attempt to answer them.

When I was a high school student, the subject that least interested me was history. I reckoned I was living in the present. I wanted to learn about what we can do in the now, I wanted to contribute to making life better in the now and in the future. This thinking changed as I added decades to my life experience. Now I study with great interest how we lived in past centuries—and in doing so, I am at times overwhelmed when I realize how far we have come. How could we ever have lived without mass and rapid transportation, without electricity, with horse carriage speed of communication, without modern medicine to rely on? Clearly, we have made huge progress! In many ways, paradise is here—but in many places it is not.

Let us look at this genre of questions from a different perspective. Let us look at it from the perspective of the **Grand Original Design** and its purpose, which we hypothesized to be the production of cosmic consciousness. I have put the word "production" intentionally not in quotation marks, because without them it sounds a bit more objective, more resolute, perhaps a bit harsher. Perhaps, in their great wisdom, the **Grand Original Designer** has been doing intentionally that which, in the big picture which we humans never see, is most proficient in reaching the desired goal. Perhaps, in the big picture, world-wide "Garden of Eden" conditions lead more to human complacency and less to true love and compassion, which are the precursors to "consciousness."

We refrain from going into further detail about this perspective and leave it up to the valued reader to pick up this thread as yet another thought experiment.

Before we move to the discussion of the subject of phenomena, which we have by now mentioned several times as being the method by which Intelligence from the other side of the veil is trying to get a hold of our attention for conveying messages, we wish to make a few remarks about our prevailing scientific research paradigm and the need for it to change.

THE NEED FOR A NEW PARADIGM
IN SCIENTIFIC RESEARCH

"A Heavenly Master governs all the world as Sovereign of the universe. We are astonished at Him by reason of His perfection, we honor Him and fall down before Him because of His unlimited power. From blind physical necessity, which is always and everywhere the same, no variety adhering to time and place could evolve, and all variety of created objects which represent order and life in the universe could happen only by the willful reasoning of its original Creator, Whom I call the Lord God."

Isaak Newton[31]

———

The scientific paradigm that is being applied at today's higher learning institutions has been the same since the time of Isaac Newton,[32] the author of the above quote. Newtonian physics, rightfully so, stands at the beginning of every course schedule in engineering and natural sciences. It is over 300 years old. It is based on the assumption that everything that is "true" must be verifiable, reproducible, without a question of a doubt. For every occurrence, for every "law" in the natural sciences, there must be a recipe, which, if precisely followed, will yield the exact same result over and over again.

Admittedly, this 300-year old scientific method works well if we are designing automobiles, buildings, or electronic equipment, or if you want to travel to the Moon or Mars or beyond. But are these "laws" applicable at the fringes of the physical reality? What if we are dealing with situations of atomic or subatomic size, and with velocities close to the speed of light? Are we simply succumbing to

---

[31] From *Azquotes.com*.

[32] Sir Isaac Newton (1643 - 1727) was an English mathematician, astronomer, theologian, author and physicist. His pioneering work, particularly in mathematics and gravity and on planetary motion, earned him the recognition of being one of the most influential scientists of all time.

the notion that there is nothing beyond those barriers, and exclude anything and everything that might exist there?

We should certainly not be doing that! In fact, modern quantum physics has been on our side for many decades. We know that, when it comes to the fringes of the physical reality, the observer of an experiment can influence the result with the power of his/her mind. Professor Dr. William A. Tiller has proven this to be true with cleverly designed experiments. We recommend his books, in particular *Psycho-Energetic Science*. Cleve Baxter,[33] the inventor of the lie detector, did stunning psycho-energetic research in the 1960s and early 70s with lie detector apparatus, which unquestionably demonstrated psycho-energetic effects.

Yet these types of experiments are being attacked by the scientific community, because they are not considered conducted in the "classical" way. We still disregard findings that cannot be fully reproduced—rather than doing just the opposite, which would be to redouble our efforts and find out why that one attempt to reproduce the results, in spite of following the recipe, did not succeed!

Let us entertain the following thought experiment: "If it is true that there is something of significance and intelligence that is beyond space and time, how would that which created everything communicate this circumstance to us? Would this communication only be through facts that we can understand, comprehend, calculate? What other kind of communication would 'They' use?"

To this day, an academic physicist will be ostracized by many of his colleagues if he openly engages in research involving unexplained phenomena. They would say, "If something cannot be explained, it is not valid." I have personally been on the offending side of this truth. When I joined the Stanford University faculty in the late 1970s, the grapevine had it that my senior colleague, Prof. Tiller—the most brilliant scientist I have ever had the privilege to personally meet—was engaged in some "weird" research. But it would remain in the

---

[33] See "Cleve Backster," in *Wikipedia*.

grapevine. We would not dare to touch the topic. It would take another quarter century, until both of us were in retirement, that we met again at a conference where he presented on his pioneering research on psycho-energetic phenomena, to a large audience open to this sort of new research.

The mindset of critics continues to be that there must eventually be a natural, scientific explanation forthcoming for an observed phenomenon, or the phenomenological experience must be considered flawed. This must change! We acknowledge that there is steady, but still only very slow, progress toward acceptance of a scientific method that embraces the unexplainable. But much more needs to be done. It is actually interesting to note that Newton himself, the person after whom the obsolete scientific method is named, was a deeply spiritual person. He saw the limitations of his discoveries, and he had no trouble in believing in a "Creator" of the universe. Yet we still experience a predominant response ranging from courteous disbelief to outright ridicule if we speak about the need for a new scientific paradigm that includes the possibility of manifestation of phenomenological communication, such as from a "Dimension of Unlimited Possibilities."

This needs to change!

4. PHENOMENA

Spirit orbs, photographic abnormalities, apparitions, crop circles, UFOs, ETs, are these all totally separate occurrences, or is there something that they have in common? We present arguments that there is a commonality between these and other phenomena, and that there is a purpose why we see them.

"Science is beautiful when it makes simple explanations of phenomena or connections between different observations."
Stephen Hawking

I consider it a miracle that I, as a trained physicist with a career in fundamental experimental physics research, most of it done at respectable institutions like NASA and Stanford University, got interested in researching subjects that cannot be explained within the conventional scientific research paradigm and, therefore, traditionally rank in the category of "meaningless anecdotal occurrences." I prefer to call these subjects "phenomena" and include a wide range of phenomenal experiences in this topic, all the way from spiritual apparitions to light phenomena, such as photographically recorded orbs, to crop circles and even UFOs, as well as to phenomenological— often called "spiritual"—healing.

Life is full of experiences that cannot be explained with conventional rationale. Everybody encounters them. I have myself witnessed many. Yet most people consider them irrelevant and live as if phenomena do not exist. They deny them, often with great zeal. Many ridicule them or those who give credence to them.

As we discussed in the preceding chapter, this attitude of "denial and despise" is a remnant of Newtonian thinking. It is not "modern." It is not fashionable— or should not be. It is an aging 300-year old paradigm. It is astonishing that the prevailing research principle which is, to this day, adhered to even in the most advanced universities is based on this antiquated paradigm that, if a scientific result cannot be predictably reproduced under careful experimental conditions, it is not considered valid.

This pertains to the orb phenomenon, crop circles, apparitions, near death experiences (NDEs), out-of-body experiences (OBEs), electronic voice perception (EVP), and even unidentified flying objects (UFOs), as well as numerous other experiences that are also falling in the general category of non-human intelligence. All of these cannot be irrefutably reproduced, and therefore the old paradigm excludes them from serious consideration. We discuss some of these phenomena in more detail in the next chapters.

It is interesting to note that, in most cases, there are groups and organizations dealing exclusively with any one—or one type—of phenomenon. We spoke, for example, at several conferences that were specifically organized around the Orb phenomenon. There were, at the time of this writing, at least 18 active international UFO organizations in 9 countries.[34] Interests in NDEs are represented by an "International Association for Near-Death Studies."[35] There are organizations that stage tours and conferences on crop circles.[36] A multitude of organizations and groups are studying spiritual apparitions. Numerous organizations are devoted to the study of Kinesiology. An organization called "Out of Body Experience Research Foundation" (OBERF)[37] reports over 3000 case studies. The list goes on and on.

All of these groupings focus narrowly on their specific phenomenon. But not much effort is being made to bring these

---

[34] See "List of UFO organizations." In *Wikipedia.*

[35] See "International Association for Near-Death Studies." In *Wikipedia*

[36] See *Cropcircleconnector.com*

[37] See http://www.oberf.org/

organizations, or at least some of them, under some sort of umbrella.[38] Presumably they are perceived as being very different from each other and having nothing in common. People may give credence to, and show interest in, some but not others. I have, for example, talked to people who had absolutely no problem with reports of physical abduction and surgeries in extraterrestrial aircraft, or of ETs living among us, but who voiced serious skepticism about the orb phenomenon.

A couple of years ago I was invited to join a working symposium of a small group of sincerely devoted people studying the UFO/ET phenomenon. The perception was that my experience in Orbs research might, perhaps, shed some light on their subject of studies. I readily agreed to join their symposium and looked forward to perhaps getting some insights in the underlying wisdom behind these phenomena, or behind phenomena at large. During the weeks leading up to the symposium I received from the organizer a sheer endless number of emails, with dozens of hours of videos by UFO/ET experiencers and researchers recommended to listen to.

All of these were pertinent and interesting, yet overwhelmingly trending in one direction—conspiracy—which I had some difficulty harmonizing with.[39] I began to doubt if there would be any openness at the meeting for the questions and concerns on my mind. Should I really attend the symposium? My conditioning—which would be politely following through with commitments I made—prevented me from outright cancelling my presentation. And then the "Universe" took care of the situation. Two days prior to the conference, totally out of the blue, I fell ill with an intestinal infection that led me to the emergency room and "medical house arrest" for the next few days, some 300 miles away from the site of the symposium.

---

[38] Rey Hernandez, FREE, is a notable exception. In his doctoral dissertation he attempted to find some commonalities among various phenomena (private communication; more references to his work follow).

[39] Most of this work was related to government cover-ups of UFO/ET evidence.

We argue further on in this book that this individualized, selective approach to phenomena may just be caused by inadequate human preconceptions, perhaps based on our personal education or conditioning. For example, crop circles are huge, while orbs are tiny. Our human conditioning, which considers physical size as a very significant discriminator, would "intuitively" treat the two as totally different—because we are trained to think this way. But if we set aside the concept of physical size, are orbs and crop circles really all that different? In what aspects are they different, and what do they have in common?

I had long been wondering if there is a commonality in all these seemingly very different phenomena, something that would lead to their veracity and their deeper meaning and purpose. Indeed, during the time between that missed UFO/ET symposium and the beginnings of writing this book, some exciting answers to these questions were intuited in my mind, and I feel privileged to communicate them at this time. In the following we present, for better understanding, first some of these phenomena, and we will then look at the commonalities and the question of meaning of it all.

4.1 ORBS - EMANATIONS FROM SPIRIT ENTITIES

"When Anthonie van Leeuwenhoek used the microscope to introduce us to bacteria and microorganisms, he opened another dimension. Now we are being introduced to yet another mysterious dimension, that of the orb. I expect this new experience will yield an even more exciting world than did the microscope. Here you will find unequaled beauty and mystery."[40]

C. Norman Shealy, M.D., Ph.D.

When, back in 2004, we began seeing intriguing circular, translucent features in our flash photographs, we started investigating what they might be. We took more and more photos, thousands of them, examined them and concluded that the vast majority of these "orb" features could not be explained as photographic abnormalities, such as reflections at particulates suspended in the air near the camera, stray-light lens reflections, camera defects, or alike, but that they warrant serious examination and consideration as phenomena.[41]

At the time, there was no substantive literature about orbs, and the Internet provided essentially no clues. We felt that we were on to something significant, but we were cautious with our interpretation, in part because I did not dare to compromise my reputation as a scientist with "preoccupation" with something that did not fit the prevailing scientific paradigm. However, this would not slow me down with careful "pseudo-scientific" research into these orbs. I coined the hypothesis that they are emanations from spirit entities ("spirit orbs"), which make use of our technological advances in photographic imaging at high sensitivity, down to single-photon resolution, and are available at low cost and thus open for use by many people.

---

[40] This is the endorsement text by Dr. Shealy of Klaus and Gundi Heinemann's 2010 book *Orbs, Their Mission and Messages of Hope.*

[41] In Appendix (D) we describe desirable conditions for orb photography.

In the ensuing years, I carefully went on collecting more and more evidence and became increasingly confident that my hypothesis of what these orbs are is holding. The circle of people with whom we talked about orb observations widened steadily and included persons as renowned as my former colleague at the Materials Science Department of Stanford University, Professor William A. Tiller.

In late 2006 my research into orbs had progressed to the point that I had prepared a draft manuscript and sent it to Cynthia Black, then president and editor-in-chief of Beyond Words Publishing, whom I had met earlier at a *Science and Consciousness* conference in Albuquerque, NM. Some three months later, I received a phone call from Cynthia. She told me that she had received a manuscript on the same subject, but quite different in the details, from a person who had been working with orbs in nature settings—ours at the time were almost exclusively in settings of spiritual-type indoor gatherings. Would I consider publishing my manuscript jointly with him?

It turned out that this other author was Dr. Miceal Ledwith, a renowned theologian who had worked for many years as a catholic priest, as department head of a theological seminary, and as Monsignor at the Vatican. Dr. Ledwith and I agreed to Cynthia's proposal, and our two manuscripts, unedited by each other, with a jointly authored introduction and conclusions section, were published soon thereafter (in 2007) as the book *The Orb Project*.[42] It has since been published in many languages, including German, Dutch, Italian, Russian, Croatian, Romanian, Japanese, and most recently in French.

Dr. Ledwith and Dr. Tiller had known each other as contributors to the acclaimed 2004 Film/documentary *What the Bleep ...?* It was therefore natural that we invited Dr. Tiller to write a foreword to *The Orb Project*. In his foreword, Tiller referenced some work on phenomena which he had previously conducted together with Dr. Stanislav O'Jack, who had taken heretofore unpublished photographs

---

[42] *The Orb Project* was published as an Atria Book by Beyond Words Publishing, a Division of Simon and Schuster.

with the solid dark plastic lens cap firmly in position on the camera lens, thus blocking all light entering the camera. We would later meet with Dr. O'Jack in person and reproduce and confirm this stunning work. Some results were later included in our second book on orbs,[43] and we also mention them in the section *Non-Trivial Photographic Phenomena* in this book.

In the years following the publication of *The Orb Project* we were literally flooded with emails and photos of readers, giving much valuable additional information and insights into the orb phenomenon. When taking all these contributions of other orb photographers into consideration, it became—essentially statistically—clear that the main commonality of all these orb appearances is evidence of a communication attempt from the "other side" with a message centering around the statement that "They" stand by our side and are intent on helping us in our lives. This eventually triggered the publication of our second book on the orb phenomenon, authored by Gundi and myself, which we fittingly titled *Orbs, Their Mission and Messages of Orbs*. It was published in 2010 by Hay House and subsequently in excellent foreign translations, including German, Japanese, Mandarin, and French.[44]

In the following paragraphs we present some details about orbs research that is beyond what has been published in these two books. They include recent findings about the importance of the interiorities of orb images, more results regarding the authenticity of orbs, and the important trend of seeing orbs in video recordings, including with surveillance cameras.

---

[43] *Orbs, Their Mission and Messages of Hope*, published by Hay House (2010).

[44] https://www.theheinemanns.net/orbproject.htm.

INTERIORITIES OF ORBS

The evidence supports the hypothesis that those non-human intelligent entities that "make" the orbs intentionally cause them to appear in whatever form they would be best noticed in the photographs, and thus their messages would most readily be discovered.

Our first encounter with orbs, back in October of 2004, occurred when Gundi and I had been asked by the Rev. Dr. Ron Roth to take photos at his retreats. Our discovery of Spirit orbs in digital photos, at a retreat center near Chicago, was to change my perception of life profoundly.[45]

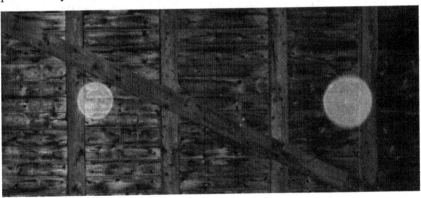

Photo 1: An orb with face (left) and another with "regular" mandala-like interiority, in the same photograph.

Among the many revelations the orb phenomenon provided to me was one about their form, or interiority. The more we examined the phenomenon, the more it became apparent to us that the Spirit entities, of which the orbs are assumed to be emanations, would design the orbs in the way which is most congenial, or most appealing, for the

---

[45] In fact, we later discovered heretofore unnoticed orbs also in digital photos we had taken at earlier retreats with Ron Roth. However, they were then small in numbers. This clearly attested to the general observation which we later published that, once detected, the number of orbs showing up in an observer's camera will quickly increase by as much as a hundredfold.

person(s) "designated" to receive them to actually see and appreciate them. For me, and also for Gundi, it was initially in the form of circles with beautiful, mandala-like interiorities. For a long time, I considered any notion that they could actually look like human faces as utter nonsense.

But then, not until 2007, after we had just published *The Orb Project*, we encountered an irrefutable face in an orb photo that showed up in my camera (see Photo 1). It was so stark that the question was no longer if it was a face, but whose face it was. We had intuitively followed the correct scientific protocol and shot a series of photos of the same scene, which enabled us to do an analysis that yielded valuable information about how orbs are formed. That orb photo did not just show this overwhelming facial feature of a person but also, right next to it, quite conveniently a "conventional" (mandala-like) orb. Comparison with the companion photos taken just prior and just subsequently, which showed no orbs at all, revealed that the intelligence behind the formation of orbs in photos made use of background image features in the design of the facial feature.[46]

Other orb experiencers would see faces immediately, and the faces they were able to see in their orb photos—I myself would sometimes be hard pressed to see any at all—would be highly significant to them.[47]

Following the publication of our books on orbs, we received multitudes of e-mails from other orb enthusiasts all over the world, and they revealed that people would often notice orbs quite different from the way we saw them; the apparent commonality was that the orbs would appear in a form in which the people involved would detect them easiest. Those who liked geometries would see orbs in geometric arrangements, such as squares, equal-sided triangles, or alike. A person with great interest in jewelry sent us a photo with

---

[46] See *Orbs, Their Mission and Messages of Hope*, pp. 64ff and Photo 54.

[47] Ibid., pp. 67ff, "Freda's Orb," Photos 55-57.

an orb in diamond-like shape in a prominent position on her arm.[48] A devout healing arts practitioner, who likes to use crystals in her practice, saw an orb in a crystal-like, hexagonal shape (Photo 2). A professional lithographer sent us a photo of an orb with letters and numbers in its interiority.[49] The list of such examples goes on and on. Clerics would see orbs with a star or a cross inside. Some people with interest in colors would see orbs in beautiful colors.

These observations confirm the hypothesis that the non-human intelligent entities that "make" the orbs might intentionally cause them to appear in whatever form would be best for the orbs to be

noticed, and thus their messages to be discovered. Clearly, the indication is that the ability of the Spirit entity who "produces" these orbs includes conscious adaptability to forms and features as they seem fit. This is by no means an expected outcome of our research – it took quite a while, and a lot of orb photos and contact with many other orb photographers, and of course intuition, to come to this conclusion.

Photo 2: Hexagonally shaped orb on a ceiling encasement of the work space of a healing arts practitioner who likes to use crystals in her practice (photo courtesy of Cindy Au, 2014).

This hypothesis is further confirmed with orbs seen in film recordings, such as taken with security cameras. We are discussing this phenomenon in a subsequent chapter entitled *Orbs in video recordings.*

---

[48] See, for example, Photo 5 in https://www.healingguidance.net/orbs.

[49] Photo 21 in https://www.healingguidance.net/orbs shows a colorful orb in high resolution with an interiority exhibiting letters and numbers. Letters S, F, I, C, V, T, O, as well as the numbers 3 and 6 are recognizable.

SOME REFLECTIONS ABOUT THE "AUTHENTICITY" OF ORBS

> We must adopt a new paradigm in scientific research, one that includes the mind – both the mind of the experiencer and the Mind at large, whatever we understand this to be.

The subject of authenticity of orb recordings is of primary importance to critics. We have addressed this subject in our previous books, including the *The Orb Project* and *Orbs, Their Mission and Messages of Hope.*

Photos 3 and 4: taken at different zoom settings, the orb-like feature is identified as lens reflection – but nonetheless meaningful (photos courtesy of A. Castellanos, 2017).

In these publications, we have intuitively assumed the following *Webster* definition of what we mean

when we talk about orb authenticity: "Worthy of acceptance or belief as conforming to, or based on, fact."[50] With regard to orbs, critics would typically consider an orb to be "authentic" only if its appearance cannot be explained with conventional wisdom that is

---

[50] This is only one of many dictionary meanings attributable to the word "authenticity," but it is presumably that which critics would use.

based on rigorous scientific examination.[51] If, for example, it can be demonstrated that an orb-like feature can be explained as due to flash reflection at a dust particle near the camera lens, or a light reflection in the camera lens, or some other plausible camera or photographic defect, this feature would then be categorized as "non-authentic." Such non-authentic orbs would be entirely discarded by these critics, and they would associate no meaning to them. In this Chapter we discuss that this criterion for authenticity of orbs is limiting and insufficient.[52] The following example describes such a situation.

After the conclusion of a profound personal spiritual experience, Tony (name changed for privacy), was photographed by a friend accompanying him. Tony noticed a colorful orb-like feature in the photo and interpreted it as a sign given to him in conjunction with what he had earlier experienced. Overjoyed about this instantaneous confirmation from another realm, he queried the Internet and contacted me as an "orb expert." He emailed me the photo, asking me for my assessment regarding the authenticity of this orb appearance (Photo 3). Unquestionably, his mind-set was based on the above described definition—he kept emphasizing how important it is for him to learn if this is, indeed, a "genuine" orb.

When I looked at the photo, I immediately suspected that, what Tony had interpreted as an orb, is in fact a lens reflection. To be able to make a more detailed analysis, I requested more photos, taken before and after this one, if available, as well as the original photo files.

It turned out that the photo was one of a series of many, all taken with a high-end digital camera. Tony flooded me with about 20 photo

---

[51] There are some critics—albeit decreasing in number---who go a step further and steadfastly state that, if we have not yet found a "natural" explanation for the particular appearance of an orb, we will certainly find one after some additional research effort. On this basis, they categorically dismiss any and all orbs as "not authentic." We do not intend to address this school of critics.

[52] It is for this reason that we have placed the word "Authenticity" in parenthesis in the chapter headline.

shots, all taken a few seconds apart. All were taken from the same perspective. Four of them showed the "orb," the others did not.

This in and by itself was suspicious. A genuine orb is usually never seen at essentially the same location in two subsequent photos. In fact, if that happens, this is usually a qualifier indicating that the orb-like feature is caused by some sort of camera or lighting defect. But then, why was the orb, which was clearly an artifact, shown in four, and not in all 20 photos?

I looked at the metadata of the photo files and found that the four photos showing the "orb" were taken at 32mm camera zoom, while all the others were identified as taken with 24-28mm zoom settings. This gave it away: it must have been a camera/light reflection effect. Of course, zoom settings in a camera lens are altered by changing the relative distances between the individual lenses that comprise the camera optics system. Therefore, light entering the camera lens from outside will be reflected at different angles when the individual lenses inside are displaced. Consequently, these light reflections will strike the photo sensor in different places, and the resulting lens diffraction effect is expected to be different at different zoom settings. This explains without a question of a doubt that, in Tony's photos, we are dealing with lens reflections and not genuine orbs. The photos taken at one zoom setting happen to show an orb-like feature, and no such peculiarity is seen at other zoom settings. The "orb" is "fake." End of story.

End of story? Really? For the skeptic, this may be so. After all, the fact is that the orb came about as a completely explainable photographic effect. There is nothing supernatural in or about it. We are not dealing with a supernatural orb phenomenon but with a simple physical lens reflection effect. Therefore, the skeptic would simply conclude that there is no meaning involved.

But this would not work for me! For me, the story is just beginning to get juicy! After having worked with the orb phenomenon for many years, my—albeit still very personal and, in the scientific community widely considered controversial—assessment is an emphatic "No, this is not the end of the story." We have just seen the top of the iceberg in terms of the questions which I submit need to be asked: "Why did Tony see that orb-like feature, just after having had his profound experience? What was it that triggered this photo to be taken, in this particular constellation, with the positions of the photographer, the sun and the window above just exactly being right to generate the orb in the photo, in just the perfect location with regard to where Tony was standing? Was it all coincidental that this particular camera was used, exactly at 32mm zoom, so that—considering the angle of the incoming sun—the orb would show? What can be deduced from the particular location of the orb with respect to Tony? Could it be that only he would know? What enticed the photographer to take so many shots, and changing the zoom, hence increasing the chance that the "correct" focal length was used that would produce the orb, just this particular orb? But not in all photos? What was behind all that? Was this all random? Or was there some guidance behind all this? Are these all irrelevant questions?"

We should never park our common sense when it comes to looking at the authenticity of phenomena. We can never get to the real results of an investigation if we shut ourselves off from asking the right questions. When it comes to the fringes of, or goes beyond, the physical reality, which is where phenomena originate, where—as modern physicists understand—an influence of the mind cannot be excluded, we must dare to ask this genre of "scientifically unusual" questions that seem irrelevant to the skeptic. We must rather adopt a new paradigm of research approach, a paradigm that includes the mind—both the mind of the experiencer and the Mind at large, whatever we understand this to be.

Given this framing in a larger context, Tony's hunch, when he first saw the "orb" in the photo—an instantaneous affirmation from another realm of his profound experience—may well be considered confirmed. And what we now know about how Entities on the other side of the veil can make use of our highly energy-sensitive equipment,[53] such as digital cameras, this photo may well have been intended to convey to Tony precisely the same message as it would have if it had been an "authentic" orb.

Even more so, the Mind that created this "orb" may well have known what would ensue, i.e., that Tony would send it to me, and that I would incorporate it into this book as an important piece of evidence that there is meaning behind phenomena even if they can be partially explained. Indeed, this is "a message worthy of acceptance."

[53] See *The Orb Project* and *Orbs, Their Mission and Messages of Hope*, as well as other books and articles summarized in http://www.healingguidance.net/orbs/ and http://www.healingguidance.net/books/.

ORBS IN VIDEO RECORDINGS

Given that the mysterious intelligence that emanates orbs onto electronic recording media is adapting to the technological trend, and given that smart phones with excellent video recording capabilities, as well as surveillance cameras, have become commonplace, it is not surprising that more and more people see orbs in video recordings. However, for various reasons orb videos seem to bear fewer possibilities for meaningful messages than still photos.

Our research into the orb phenomenon that led to the publication of our books *The Orb Project* and *Orbs, Their Mission and Messages of Hope* was based on conventional still photography with point-and-shoot digital cameras. It wasn't until several years later that more and more people would leave their point-and-shoot camera at home and rely on their smart phone for photography. Unfortunately, the weaker flash of smart phones, when compared to dedicated digital photo cameras, impacted orb photography.

More recently, the technical advancement and pricing reduction of smartphones and, in particular, video surveillance cameras further enticed people to purchase such video recording equipment, and people started seeing orb phenomena recorded with them. It is almost as if "regular" still photography of orbs is being replaced with video recordings of orbs, or, as we would rephrase, "The entities emanating orbs onto electronic recording media are adapting to the technological trend and more and more often use orb video recordings to make people aware of the existence and significance of a reality beyond the physical realm."

In increasing numbers, orb enthusiasts are now sending us video recordings from surveillance cameras that show authentic orbs in motion. We have confirmed these observations ourselves and obtained stunning film clips of this twist of the orb phenomenon, recorded both with our iPhone and with a surveillance camera installed at our home.

Photos 5: Series of five snapshots from a video recording showing a moving orb, taken with a security camera at our home. Each photo represents one (cropped) frame from that

movie clip, in about one-second intervals. It is apparent that during this short time the orb never moved in a continuous motion but rather always in a quantum step-wise fashion. Below: typical full picture frame. (Recorded on 12/5/16).

Security surveillance cameras are inherently infra-red (IR) sensitive, which also happens to be the favored light frequency range for imaging orbs. In the example shown in *Photos 5*, the security camera is mounted such that it overlooks our parking area, behind an entrance gate. On the left side it looks at a house corner, which is about 6 feet from the camera location. The camera has a built-in IR light source, which preferentially illuminates the house wall facing the camera—hence that wall appears bright. We are examining a representative film clip. Within a recording of a few seconds, an orb is moving seemingly erratically in various directions throughout the entire field of view, back and forth and up and down. We are showing five snapshots of the multitude of momentary locations of the orb. The field of view is slightly cropped.

Not shown in the sequence of photos depicted above is an indication that the orb may have actually disappeared behind the house wall on the left in the field of view of the camera, presumably entering into the room behind, and re-emerged to the open space on the other side of the house corner.[54] The large picture in *Photos*

[54] This can be seen at http://www.theheinemanns.net/Moving-Orbs.mp4. Here we have shown and annotated the video itself. First, the entire relevant portion

5 shows the entire field of view of the camera, depicting a moment when the orb was just disappearing into the wall (shown just below the two incidental wire strings that happen to be holding a bush in the foreground in position and have no relation to this phenomenon).

The reader may appreciate that it is generally very difficult to present the essence of a movie clip in printed media, where only still-photos can be shown. However, a movie picture is composed of a multitude of separate individual picture frames (typically 30 per second), and it is therefore possible to select and print certain picture frames from a movie clip at will to make a point. In our example in *Photos 5* we have tried to depict the most representative movie frames for showing a particular displacement event of the orb. Our 4th and 5th frames actually show the orb while in motion. These movie frames are directly comparable to "conventional" still photographs with orbs, in which we, and other orb photographers, have previously observed and described orbs in motion.

These still photographs, or movie picture frames in this case, show the orb not all smeared or out of focus in the direction of motion, but rather in clear, in-focus discrete dislocations. The orb is not moving gradually and continually, but it is being displaced from one position to the next, then pauses, then "jumps" to the next position, and pauses gain, all happening during the short duration of recording of the picture frame (about 1/30th of a second).

Before we discuss this "quantum-step" like motion process of orbs in the following chapter, let us look at the energetics of recording orbs in videos, as compared to still photographs. Here we need to differentiate between videos taken with dedicated video cameras (or smart phones), and with surveillance cameras. The difference is

---

of the video is shown; then the same is presented in 50% slower motion, then in further reduced motion, and finally in extremely slow motion (40 times slower than original). However, as we mention later in this book, image processing of this orb's movement casts some doubt about the veracity of disappearance behind, and re-appearance from, the wall. More research on this particular behavior of orbs would be desirable.

mainly determined by two parameters: the wavelength of the photons (light) used in the imaging process, and the intensity of the scene illumination provided during filming in the night vision mode.

Regular cameras, as well as smart phones, respond to light in the visible wavelength range (approximately 400-700 nm). Surveillance cameras operating in night vision mode work at about twice that wavelength (about 850 nm), i.e., in the near infrared spectral range which is invisible to the human eye. We estimate from our research into still photography of orbs that it takes about a few hundred photons, which is an energy equivalent of the order of 10^{-16} Watt-seconds, to produce a rudimentary orb image on a photographic charge plate.[55] Since infrared photons are less energetic than photons in the visible range, this means that, apart from every other consideration, surveillance cameras require less energy to record an orb image than smart phone-type cameras. It is believed that the conscious nonphysical entities which produce the orbs are doing so by beaming photons into the recording camera, and that they typically do this by converting energy coming from the camera flash. Since surveillance cameras require less energy to record an orb on their photo sensor, they are energetically preferable instruments for orb visualization.

However, we should mention here that the conscious nonphysical entities assumed to be "producing" spirit orbs are, in principle, well capable of generating more energy, and they will "gladly" do so if they so choose. They are, for example, known to occasionally produce very large orbs with intricate interiorities that take orders of magnitude more photons to record than just a few hundred photons which we had assumed to be required for recording small, faint, nondescript orbs. In extreme cases, we know that large, high-contrast orbs with mandala-like interiorities have even been recorded on conventional emulsion-type film,[56] which is much less light sensitive

---

[55] Heinemann, Klaus. "The Orb Phenomenon: Bridging to the World Beyond?" *Light, Vol 134, No 1, Spring 2013.*

[56] For example, the professional Dutch photographer Ed Vos recorded numerous intricate orb photos on conventional photographic emulsion film.

than the CCD image charge plates used in electronic cameras and requires substantially more photon energy per recording.

It is, as described above, a well-known conclusion from overwhelming evidence that orbs can be produced much easier—albeit not exclusively—when external energy is provided during the photographic event. This usually occurs by means of a flash in still photography, or a strobe light or simply a bright continuous illumination in video filming. Let us now look at the illumination characteristics that are typically available for recording orbs with point-and-shoot cameras and compare this with those of movie cameras. Are the energies of flashes, or strobe lighting, and continuous lighting comparable?

First, we compare the illumination energy that is required for flash still-photography with the illumination typically available in film and surveillance cameras. A camera flash is very bright but typically lasts only about $1/1000^{th}$ of a second. During this short time, it will illuminate the photographed scene quite intensely. The shutter will be open much longer, usually about $1/60^{th}$ sec, and with proper synchronization the flash event will fall into that time interval. The actual photo imprint on the camera charge plate is dependent on the total amount of light reflected from the illuminated scene, not the momentary brightness, i.e., it is mathematically described by the integral of the brightness over time. In flash photography, even though the shutter is open for a much longer time, all the exposure is done in that short 1/1000 sec interval of the actual flash illuminance. During the entire rest of the $1/60^{th}$ sec shutter opening time, the photographed scene is black and will essentially not contribute to the photo recording.

What this all means is that a steady light illumination at a brightness of just a small fraction of the intensity of a flash[57] will, in principle, provide the same illuminance, and hence the same image result, as typical camera flash. Therefore, in order to be able

---

[57] Provided that the spectrum of both light sources is the same.

to record orbs in smart phone movie clips, one would either need strobe lighting (a synchronized flash activated thirty times per second during filming), or simply a regular, continuous lighting source illuminating the object. State-of-the-art smart phones provide such a steady lighting source.[58] Therefore, it is in principle understandable that one can see orbs in video recordings.

This is not self-evident. Before I had gone through this rationale, I had intuitively assumed that, when people see orbs in videos, they were seeing a different kind of orbs, or a somewhat different orb phenomenon. Instead, there is a direct, 1:1 correlation between orbs seen in still photos and in videos.

Now let us look at the illumination situation in the case of infrared ("IR") cameras, such as in typical surveillance cameras. Again, the illumination is at constant brightness. The IR emission is provided by powerful light emitting diodes ("LEDs") working in the near infrared wavelength range (about 850 nm). These emitters are very bright and provide an illuminance reaching quite far, certainly extending further than the typical light source in a high-quality smart phone. Yet the IR illumination is essentially not detectable with the human eye, which has a detection limit at around 700 – 750 nm. It is, therefore, logical that surveillance cameras are good, or even better instruments for detection of moving orbs than smart phones.

All this explains why an IR-sensitive surveillance camera is equally, or even better, "qualified" to record orbs in videos than a point-and-shoot still camera can record orbs in photos. And it explains why a regular smart phone, which has only a relatively weak built-in light source for illumination of a scene when shooting a video under extremely low light conditions, records videos with orbs much more seldom than an IR sensitive surveillance camera. Given that nowadays surveillance cameras have become almost as

---

[58] However, the actual brightness of a smart phone lighting source, or a smart phone flash, is much inferior to the brightness of the flash of a typical point-and-shoot camera, which is why the latter devices produce much better orb photos than the former.

much commonplace as digital point-and-shoot cameras were in 2004, when we first discovered orbs in our photos, it is, therefore, not surprising that more and more people report seeing orbs in their video recordings.

The question then remains how we can interpret orbs in video recordings. From our work with orbs in still photography we concluded that it is positioning of the orb in the photo that is predominantly used by the entities emanating the orbs for communicating a message. How would the entities convey their messages via moving orbs? What kind of messages can they easily communicate in orb videos?

We are only at the very beginning of tackling this question. Clearly, the important aspect of interpreting messages from the positioning of orbs in a photo does not apply in videos. Here the orbs move all over the scene, mostly in entirely erratic patterns. It is conceivable that they might move in the pattern of "writing" numbers, letters, or symbols; but it is cumbersome to meaningfully trace the movement of an orb even in a stationary movie scene, and people would not normally have the patience and/or the experimental means for this kind of evaluation. We have attempted such analyses but have not been able to get results that look encouraging. More work would have to be done to ascertain such a communication pattern.

Another method of evaluating still orb-photography is communication via the interiority of imaged orbs. As we explained earlier, this would also be difficult to apply to orb videos, primarily for energetic reasons. To produce orbs with descriptive interiorities takes many more photons, i.e., much more energy to accomplish than what is required for recording small, featureless orbs. Translating this to videos, the additional amount of energy would have to be expended not only once but to hundreds of image frames during the duration of the orb appearance in the video. In the orb videos which we have observed and attempted to evaluate, any one single orb movement event lasted from about 0.5 to over 5 seconds. The energy required to "write" a five-second long orb trail in a video amounts to several hundred times the energy required for a single orb photo. It is certainly possible to do this even with highly intricate orbs, but not very likely. It is more probable that we will see featureless moving orbs, just small opaque disks with uniform interiority.

Furthermore, the image resolution of surveillance cameras in the night vision mode is significantly inferior to that of typical point and shoot cameras. Even if the orb had an intricate interiority, the surveillance camera would likely not be able to resolve those features.

If the surveillance camera is, as is the case in the video we analyzed earlier in this chapter, mounted such that it looks at a house corner, a unique feature becomes feasible to study. One may be able to observe an orb disappearing into the wall and re-emerging into the field of view from the other side, just as if there were no wall impeding its path of movement. This would, in and by itself, be confirmation that physical objects are no impediments for orbs, which in turn could be taken as confirmation of our hypothesis that orbs have no electromagnetic properties and cannot be explained with conventional laws of physics. This would give further credence to the assumption that a world around us exists where conscious, highly evolved beings dwell that are fundamentally different from us in one important aspect: they have no physicality.

We have extensively investigated several videos recorded with the particular surveillance camera that looks at a house corner, including the film strip of about 15 seconds length from which we selected the still shots shown in *Photos 5* earlier in this chapter. That same orb appears to have entered into the wall and exited on the other side not once but actually several times during the duration of the film clip. However, this particular result, even though observed in several film clips, is preliminary and calls for further documentation.

As a further remark regarding orb recordings with surveillance cameras we should mention that some cameras are designed to record in a time laps mode. Rather than recording thirty image frames per second, as is the norm for videos, they are programmed to record a smaller number of frames per second and to ignore and delete the empty frames in-between those that actually get recorded, thus saving valuable data storage resources. This renders the paths of moving orbs choppy and even less "useful," or more difficult to evaluate.

In conclusion, seeing orbs in videos is the trend of the time. However, for various reasons, including technical considerations, orb videos seem to bear fewer possibilities for conveying meaningful messages than still photos. We therefore encourage the reader who desires to receive messages from the other side of reality via the orb phenomenon to continue to do this with single frame photography, preferably using a dedicated point and shoot camera, rather than a smart phone.[59]

---

[59] See Appendix (D), where we give specific recommendations with regard to the type of camera that would be best suited for dedicated orb photography.

ORBS "PAINTING" FAIRY-LIKE FEATURES

A high degree of consciousness stands behind that which generates spirit orb images. With quantum-step like displacement in very rapid succession, orbs can even "paint" fairy-like images for convenient recognition by those whose attention can preferably be reached by such features.

After the publication of *The Orb Project* in 2007, Gundi and I were invited to a presentation of our findings at a conference on orbs and crop circles in Germany. It was at an orb photography event during that conference that I was, for the first time, introduced to the fact that meaningful orbs can show in other than circular shapes. *Photo 1* (in Chapter 4.1, *Interiorities of Orbs*) was taken at that occasion. Earlier in the day, at that conference, two speakers presented about "fairies" and similar creatures they thought they had seen in their phenomena photographs. I remember that I was sitting there, perplexed, not quite sure if I should demonstratively walk out of the meeting room or otherwise make my disagreement about this "nonsense" known. Fortunately, I ended up doing neither.

Four years later, in 2011, I found out why, and how, those pictures of fairies could arise and make sense after all. An Austrian friend sent us a perplexing photo with a large, fairy-like feature for evaluation. I cropped and contrast-enhanced it, and *Photo 6* resulted.

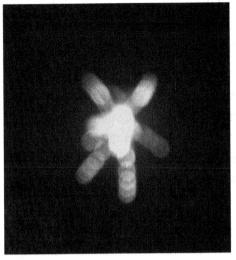

Photo 6: This figure (cropped and enlarged) was "painted" during the 1/60 second camera exposure, using a 1/1000 second flash, presumably by one orb, with about 50 quantum step displacements. (Photo courtesy of Titica, Graz, Austria, 2011).

Upon close examination of what looked like some sort of fairy (*Photo 6*) is not really a fairy at all but rather an image of a moving target— one single orb "painting" a picture that looks like a fairy. Our interpretation of this photo has been that the entity in the unseen reality, which "designed" and executed the orb in the photo, may have wanted to impress the photographer of this remarkable image with an orb in the form which she wanted to see, i.e., as a "fairy."

Titica got what she asked for! Her photo is one of many photographic evidences we have in our files showing that the Entities emanating orb images are perfectly capable and willing to adapt the shapes and interiorities of their orbs in such a way that they are most readily noticed by those whom they want to reach with this information. A person who would want to see a face will receive an orb with a face (see *Photo 1*); an author intrigued by letters and words might see an interiority containing letters; a healing arts practitioner working with crystals might see an orb in hexagonal outer shape (*Photo 2*); and a person who is fascinated with gnomes and fairies and alike might receive an orb image like the one in *Photo 6*.

The conclusion that this fairy-like feature was produced by one single moving orb was not the only epiphany we obtained from examining this photo. Contrast enhancement revealed that this "painting" process was not done by continuous movement of the orb, but by stepwise displacements of the one orb that generated the figure. We can see as many of fifty quantum step-like displacements.

They all occurred during the 1/60 sec shutter opening and—more astonishingly—"fueled" by the 1/1000 sec camera flash while the shutter was open.

Again, this indicates that there is a high degree of consciousness behind that which generates spirit orb images. As we have mentioned in various places in our orb-related publications, such quantum-step like movement of orbs has also repeatedly been noted in "regular," less stunning orb photos than Titica's. We have received similar photos showing "fairies" from other orb enthusiasts. And we have seen from our evaluation of moving orbs recorded with surveillance cameras that orbs do not move in a continuous fashion but in discrete, quantum-like displacements.

4.2 OTHER PHENOMENA

"From the point of view of basic physics, the most interesting phenomena are, of course, in the new places, the places where the rules do not work - not the places where they do work!"　　　　　　　　　　**Richard P. Feynman**

———

Among the many responses from readers of our books and articles on orbs were also numerous photos and inquiries regarding other photographic abnormalities, as well as non-photographic phenomena. As we have already mentioned in the preceding paragraphs, many of the photographic phenomena that are similar to orbs can be explained as sun reflections, or camera or operating deficiencies. Others are truly astonishing and cannot readily be explained.

In this chapter we are addressing some phenomena that can indeed be explained as photographic "artifacts"—lens reflections—but that have, nonetheless, a signature of noteworthy profundity. We then offer some thought to what we have earlier[60] called the "O'Jack Phenomenon." This is an entirely unexplained photographic phenomenon where the author, Dr. Stanislav O'Jack,[61] has taken, repeatedly and verified, photographs while the black plastic lens cap was firmly in place on the camera lens.

We conclude this chapter with some words about apparitions.

---

[60] In Appendix C of *Orbs, Their Mission and Messages of Hope.*

[61] Dr. O'Jack is also the author of the foreword of this book.

There is non-human intelligence all around us that is capable and eager to use our highly light sensitive digital cameras and record with them phenomenological pictures that have special meaning for those who take the photos, or for those who are shown in them.

One of our seminar participants, a professional Silicon Valley engineer, sent us a photo with the face of a puma, simply stating, "The puma is my power symbol." Yet another seminar participant presented a photo with phenomenal light features emanating from her mouth. She is a singer.

Photo 7: This phenomenological power animal appeared in a photo of a participant in a healing arts seminar taught by Gundi. While not in any way related to orb photography, this is an unexplainable result of photographic lens reflections. (Photo courtesy of Dr. Erich Hunter, https://www.pendulumhealing.com/, August 2014).

Photo 8: taken of a jubilant singer in a very special moment. Optical lens reflections can perhaps explain some of the features of this phenomenological photo, but not nearly everything. (Photo courtesy of Cindy Au, 2014; taken on 1/6/2004).

These two photographs are further examples of "meaningful lens reflections."[62] Indeed, the single most prevalent type of non-genuine orb photos we have received over the years from readers of our books are lens reflections that were mistaken for "real" orbs. In many of these cases, the interiority of the orb-like features, and/or their location in the photos, combined with the description of the circumstances under which the photos were taken, signified anything but random coincidence. Many of such "simple" lens reflection photos can rightfully be interpreted as if they were genuine orb photos.

In our understanding, there is no question that the spiritual entities behind orbs do indeed have the ability to make themselves known to us human observers in a great variety of ways. The two examples we showed above prove this point in that they go far beyond the regular kind of lens reflections that are normally observable in

---

[62] See also the earlier section entitled *Some Reflections About the "Authenticity" of* Orbs.

photos. While there is no doubt in my mind that lens reflections were the operating photographic mechanism in these photos, the detailed image that they actually produced cannot be explained with logical reflection geometries. No matter how much creative thinking one would apply, the image of a puma simply cannot result from angles and orientations of surfaces inside of a camera lens. And it is hard to fathom that the intricate figure at the mouth of the singer, showing what resembles a soprano note clef used when writing music, with an arrow pointing precisely toward the vocal cords of the singer, and fanning out as if one could actually see the sounds, might have come about just randomly. Who will refute that there is thought and meaning behind such phenomena?!

In *Orbs, their Mission and Messages of Hope* we already presented an example of truly extraordinary photos taken by Dr. Stanislav O'Jack with a conventional photo camera on conventional celluloid emulsion film, whereby the black, totally opaque (about 1mm thick) plastic lens cap was positioned firmly in place on the camera lens. Prior to taking the lens-capped photos, from a multitude of which one is shown in *Photo 8*, I myself had examined the camera and the lens cap and inserted the newly purchased genuine Kodak color-negative film into it. There was nothing at all unusual about any of this. Then, on that same afternoon, on a leisurely walk at Sea Ranch, CA, Stanislav[63] took all of the 24 photos of this film roll in our presence, in the same manner that you and I would take photos – except with the lens cap firmly positioned on the camera lens.

No less than 16 of the photos of this color negative film roll, all taken in complete darkness due to the lens cap firmly positioned on the lens, turned out bright and colorful, with no apparent indication of any abnormality. Just a few of Dr. O'Jack's photo exposures turned

---

[63] Dr. Stanislav O'Jack is, in terms of scientific integrity, above any reproach. He had an illustrious career as an engineer and had also worked extensively with Professor William Tiller of Stanford University, who is renowned for his own fascinating research into psycho-energetic phenomena.

out black, as one would have expected for all photos taken under these circumstances.

Photo 9: Taken in August, 2009, by Dr. Stanislav O'Jack with his conventional fixed-lens point-and-shoot camera on regular Kodak color print emulsion film, inside the Sea Ranch Chapel (showing, f.r.t.l.: his wife Helen O'Jack, Gundi Heinemann, and Klaus Heinemann). This photo was taken while the entirely opaque, about 1mm thick black plastic lens cap was firmly and tightly seated on the camera objective lens. The entire film was developed and printed by Kodak, and I then took a digital photo of the paper print.

I recall that, when I later looked at the developed film, I noticed in a couple of instances that the film had been exposed beyond the precise 24x36 mm film window all the way into the perforation. This, of course, is equally phenomenal in and by itself, but it is the only "abnormality" we noted; the color photos taken this way were otherwise entirely indistinguishable from any normal color photos one would have taken that afternoon with any good camera: no distortions, no evidence of unusual exposure, perfect sharpness and contrast, no color deviations.[64]

---

[64] In Appendix C of *Orbs, Their Mission and Messages of Hope* we present a phenomenological explanation how a photo taken under such lens-capped conditions could have come about: it would require a form of light which we know from physics does not exist in our world.

We can only scratch the surface when it comes to photographic recordings of phenomena, and present *Photos 6-8* just as examples. They are placeholders for many serious photos of this nature in our digital records, and perhaps of many thousands of people world-wide who have recorded phenomenological photos.

Our conclusion is: "There is non-human intelligence within and all around us that is capable of using our highly light sensitive digital cameras and record with them phenomenological pictures that have special meaning for those who take such photos, or for those who are shown in them. The evidence overwhelmingly indicates that there is a lot more wisdom behind these images than what could be explained as coincidental, anecdotal photographic abnormalities. It is up to us, as recipients of such images, to interpret the messages imparted to us by means of these photos."

Photos like these have changed my personal paradigm of approaching my understanding of the laws of our physical reality. As a scientist, I was trained to rigorously believe in the conventional scientific principle, which in essence states that an experiment must be fully repeatable any number of times to be trustworthy—it must be fully reproducible. If a repetition fails, we must be able to fully explain the failure or exception, or the entire experiment must be declared as failed. The new paradigm would require just the opposite. We would have to chase after the failed experiment with redoubled effort, suspecting exceptional importance in that which we cannot explain, more so than in that which is fully explainable and reproducible.

CROP CIRCLES

"Science in the true sense of the word is open to unbiased investigation of any existing phenomena." **Stanislav Grof**

The first time we heard the word "crop circle" was at a keynote presentation by Freddy Silva at the 2006 International Conference on Science and Consciousness in Santa Fe, NM. Mr. Silva described in great detail this phenomenon. For unexplained reasons, crops are found kinked in interesting patterns of up to several hundred yards in size. This has been observed in various countries all over the world, but predominantly in the cornfields around the small town of Avebury in Southern England.

Photos 10: Walking in a crop circle near Avebury, UK. Note the precise delineation of fallen and standing grains (top); and note the whirlwind-like bending pattern, occurring at nodal points of the stems (left).

Mr. Silva presented scientific evidence for authenticity of crop circles. This includes that the kinking of the grain stems occurs a few inches above grade, rather than at grade. He pointed out that fake crop circles can also occasionally be found, but in those usually primitive hoaxes the kinking does, indeed, occur at the point where the stems emerge from the soil, as one would expect if some sort of stampeding was used to "manufacture" them.

Two years later, in 2008, Gundi and I walked for the first time in crop circles in corn fields near Avebury, UK. We had traveled to an international conference on *Orb Phenomena* in Glastonbury and took a couple of day trips to near-by crop circle sites. We saw with our own eyes how perfectly a genuine crop circle is made. The two we walked in (*Photos 9*) had elements with small and big circular shapes, linear borders, and rectangular patterns of different sizes. We were intrigued how precisely one grain at a border was proudly standing, and the one next to it, and thousands beyond, were lying kinked, parallel to the ground, kinked not at grade, as one would intuitively expect, but a few inches above grade. Standing and kinked, in a perfectly circular curvature, or in a perfectly straight line! Not one kinked or standing on the respective other side!

Opinions that crop circles simply "cannot be authentic" have been loud and persistent. None other than the biologist Dr. Rupert Sheldrake, who later attained reputation for his pioneering work on morphic resonance, was, back in 1991, so adamantly critical about crop circles—convinced that all must be man-made—that he organized a "crop circle making" competition.[65] The project was successful in that it demonstrated that crop circles can indeed be hoaxed, but the scientific consensus appears to remain that a nontrivial fraction of the crop circles that continue to appear annually are unexplained, i.e., real. But unquestionably, fake and real crop circles are distinguishable. We saw them both. The one we show in *Photos 9* was not man made! Whatever produced it did something truly perplexing. Of course, there are skeptics everywhere; but I suppose seeing this amazing phenomenon with your own eyes would

---

[65] Rupert Sheldrake, *The Crop Circle Making Competition*. In 1992, John Michell and Rupert Sheldrake helped organize an *International Competition*, attempting to prove that crop circles even with intricate patterns could be man-made.

make it hard to debunk it as a "natural oddity," even if you are a staunch skeptic.

We also walked in a fake crop circle and experienced the difference first-hand. That man-made "crop circle" was nothing but a circular area of about 100 feet in diameter where all grains were flattened at grade—not above grade at the first nodes—and in disorderly orientation—not in the superb orderly directions in which the grains of the genuine crop circles we had walked in were kinked. Also, in all fairness, it must have been a far cry down from the quite impressive crop circles made by Sheldrake and his buddies in the contest back in 1992.

The episodes of having been able to walk in several crop circles in 2008 and 2009 have by no means made us experts in that particular field of phenomena research. But our expertise in Orb phenomena has given us some basis for looking at crop circles from the perspective of the energetics that might be employed to produce them, and possibly of the purpose underlying the phenomenon.

We know that it takes only a few hundred photons, i.e., minute amounts of physical energy, to record an orb in a digital photo, while crop circles are comparatively huge down-to-earth physical structures, up to several hundred meters in size. How are they made? Numerous theories have been advanced to explain this phenomenon. Before I add another one to them, let's first recall the most important features of genuine crop circles, as we have experienced them:

■ They are precise! Whatever feature they are showing, it is perfectly executed. Perfectly geometrical, perfectly mathematical, indicating that there is not only a clear mind at work, but also perfect ability to execute the design. Sometimes they are of such intricate design that a photograph taken from above, such as from an airplane or a drone, is the only way to bring out all features.

- It takes a very short time to make them. In most cases, when people have tried to be present during the making of a crop circle, they report that at first there was nothing, and in another moment later the crop circle was there. They would usually state that they "missed" what actually happened due to "inattentiveness."

- The grains that are kinked to make the crop circle interiority are not randomly folded over, but in beautiful, often circular patterns, as if formed by a small, localized whirlwind.

- Probably most significantly, one finds that in a genuine crop circle the stems of the grains are not kinked at the logical place, which would be at the point where they come out of the ground, like what would happen if you step in a grain field, but at a point a few inches above grade. We have witnessed ourselves, unmistakably, how our feet "completed" the kinking with every step we took in a crop circle. Our weight would then bend them completely at the point where they come out of the ground, as one would expect. Actually, the genuine kinking which occurs a few inches above grade are no kinks at all—upon close examination they look much more like bends, fine, relatively sharp bends at a small radius (perhaps 5 - 10mm), leaving the cylindrical structure of the grain undamaged—not actually kinked, but rather just bent.

How can we cover these four crop circle characteristics with a plausible explanation? We have argued that Orbs are imprinted on digital photo charge plates by non-human intelligent entities that have the ability of "producing" subtle energies of the order of 10^{-16} Ampere-seconds and directing those as seems fit. Might it be conceivable that these same non-human intelligent entities that make orbs are also capable of directing these minute energies to bend the stems of grains in the making of crop circles? Could these subtle energies be applied to the biological grain cells to alter the programming of the cells of the grain stems that need to be bent, locally and in such a way that these grains physically weaken and bend precisely at the intended locations?

Location and speed are of no concern in the reality where that happens.[66] Not being limited by space and time, they would be able to do this with super-luminous speeds, one grain at a time, hundreds of thousands in a moment! With highest precision. In the most amazing patterns.

This hypothetical mechanism is essentially identical to what we have hypothesized as mechanism for spiritual healing, except that, obviously, the object of the healing action is very different. We will get back to this important analogy in the chapter on *Spiritual Healing* and leave you now with the intriguing question if there might be an intentional connection between the two:

"Might one of the reasons for the appearance of crop circles be to communicate that physical healing is what the unseen reality is not only capable of, but actually actively doing?"

---

[66] See *Expanding Perception*, Chapter 2.

> We can logically conclude that, given the skill available in the realm of non-human intelligence, it is possible to energetically imprint distinct patterns in the mind of people – just as easily as it would be to imprint orbs on a photographic charge plate, or affect kinking in grains in the making of crop circles, or make cell programming corrections in human tissue in the process which we call "spirit-directed healing."

Back in 2005, Ron Roth mailed me a little booklet and asked me to read it and give him my assessment. It was about something I had never heard of prior to that time, about the apparitions at Medjugorje.[67] Ron mentioned that he visited Medjugorje several times over the preceding years and was deeply impressed about what he experienced there. I started reading the book and was immediately intrigued. It talked about something that, at the onset, made little sense to me. But it was written in an objective, factual/scientific language that appealed to me, authored by an unusual team of a theologian (René Laurentin) and a medical professional (Henri Joyeux).

Apparitions are phenomena that appear visually or audibly to certain people but not to others. They are usually not reproducible and will not normally appear in videos, photos, or audio-recordings. In *Orbs, Their Mission and Messages of Hope* we describe an apparition in the form of an orb that visibly appeared to an orb enthusiast and stayed with her for the better part of two hours. For the experiencer, this was a very real occurrence, even though she had no witness who actually saw the apparition.[68]

---

[67] *Scientific and Medical Studies on the Apparitions at Medjugorje,* by René Laurentin, and Henri Joyeux, 1986 (Veritas Publications; First English Language Edition (December 31, 1987).

[68] Described in *Orbs, Their Mission and Messages of Hope,* p. 75. There was, however, a witness of a different kind, a person whom she called on her cell phone and to whom she narrated the entire proceedings – lasting about two hours – as it was developing. This person "witnessed" the realness and the details of the

There have been many apparitions of Mother Mary, the most famous ones arguably occurred at *Fátima, Lourdes*, and more recently *Medjugorje*. In June 1981, six children in the essentially unknown village of Medjugorje in what is now the small country of Bosnia and Herzegovina began to experience something very unusual: the "Blessed Virgin" appeared to them near the altar of the village church, mostly at regular times, usually at an early evening hour. They would perceive her as a real, live person. They reported that they would see her, hear her, ask her questions, and the "Blessed Mother" would hear their questions and answer by talking to them, and they would deliver messages from her to their parents and parishioners.

These experiencers, called "visionaries," all children ages 10 and up, were reported as claiming that there was nothing really extraordinary about these apparitions. For them it was something very natural. They were—and this is important—as innocent, unbiased, and impartial as one can expect of young children growing up in a small, rural village in a generally impoverished region of what was then communist Yugoslavia. Nevertheless, and understandably, the experiences quickly came to notoriety, and clerics and critics alike "pilgrimaged" to Medjugorje in large numbers to experience the phenomenon first-hand.

Medjugorje is now a famous unofficial place of Catholic pilgrimage—still "unofficial," because the final decision by the Vatican is still out[69] whether the Catholic Church will recognize the apparitions as "valid." Indeed, criticism emerged almost immediately when the news of the apparitions was spreading back in 1981. Among the harshest critics were traditional Roman Catholic clergy. It would not take long before scientists proposed to make serious authenticity tests on these children. Among them were René Laurentin and Henri Joyeux who ended up writing their report in form of the small

---

apparition as described, but to a critic this is nonetheless nothing more than "hearsay."

[69] For details see: "Catholic Church response to the Medjugorje apparitions." In *Wikipedia*.

book which Ron Roth gave me to read, some 20 years after its first publication.

Their book describes in detail how scientists wired these kids up and measured their brain wave reactions/stimulations during the apparitions. They found that the scientifically measured responses were essentially identical to those which we as normal people generate when we see, hear, and communicate—all this while there was nothing visible or audible to bystanders. Unmistakably, the actual perception by the experiencer children was not through their physical ears and eyes, but it was authentically registered with their senses nonetheless. To this day, I consider this book to be authentic, in particular also because it is authored jointly by a scientist and a cleric, and I recommend it to those readers who are interested in following up on the interesting topic of the Apparitions of Medjugorje.

In the summer of 1916, three shepherd children, 6, 8, and 9 years of age, in the province of Fátima, Portugal, reported that they were visited by an "Angel of Peace." In the following year, several more visitations occurred. Two of the experiencer children died in the international flue pandemic in 1918. The third lived to report about the details of the apparitions. She became known as Sister Lúcia. She had several additional significant apparitions in the following 23 years. Sister Lúcia died in 2005 at age 97.

The teachings of the visions were very significant but go beyond the scope of this book.[70] What we consider relevant for the discussion of apparitions as a phenomenon is that the Apparitions of Fátima appear to have occurred in a fashion quite similar to the Apparitions of Medjugorje; but, of course, no scientific testing was done, because at the time that technology was not available.

----

[70] For information about the contents of these apparitions, the reader may wish to consult: "Our Lady of Fátima." In *Wikipedia*.

We had heard so much about Lourdes that, when we were on vacation in the Provence, Southern France, in June, 2002, we decided in the spur of a moment to check out of our hotel near Avignon a couple of days early and drive the 500km to Lourdes to see what it is all about. The next day, a Saturday, saw us on what felt like the hottest day ever recorded – well over 40 C – in our small rental car, without air conditioning and continually at the brink of engine overheating when we topped 120 km/h on the mostly empty *autoroutes*, on our way to the first pilgrimage site ever we were about to visit.

When we got closer to our destination, we understood why the freeways were so empty: it wasn't that people stayed home because it was so hot, it rather felt like everybody had already arrived and congregated—in Lourdes. The masses of people were overwhelming. And then we experienced the first miracle: we found a place to park, not too far from a kiosk that dealt with hotel reservations, and after just a few minutes in line we had the booking receipt for a modest hotel room. And so, nothing was impeding our joyful exploration of the sites of this popular pilgrimage destination.

Lourdes became a pilgrimage site after 14-year old *Marie-Bernarde Soubirous* received several widely acclaimed apparitions of the Virgin Mary starting in 1858. Marie-Bernarde was canonized as *Saint Bernadette* in 1933 by Pope Pius XI. Eight years after the apparition experience at the famous Grotto in Lourdes, Bernadette was admitted as a nun at the *Convent of St. Gildard* in Nevers, central France, where she succumbed to tuberculosis at the early age of 34 in 1879.

The fascinating details of St. Bernadette's life, and her visions and the impact they had are well documented in literature.[71] Of interest to us here is that, once again, her visions apparently occurred in a very

---

[71] Actually, three years prior to our travel to Lourdes, Gundi and I participated in a "Sacred Sites" tour with Ron Roth, which included a visit of the Convent in Nevers (Espace Bernadette Soubirous), where Father Ron Roth celebrated a special mass at the Shrine of the undecomposed St. Bernadette. Our visit to Lourdes closed a loop of personal experiences.

similar fashion than those of the handful of children in Medjugorje. The apparitions appeared only to her, in a very real way, involving her visual and audio senses but not her eyes and ears, and the messages were profound and contemporary. The visions were so real to Bernadette that she steadfastly defended their authenticity to skeptical emissaries from the pope who tried to convince her otherwise. This went on for years. Even in her final hour she is said to have insisted to nagging representatives of the Vatican that it was real.

There have been hundreds of apparitional experiences reported in literature, dating back to the middle ages. I presume that the three I have addressed in this chapter are more or less representative of the general "mechanical" circumstances pertaining to most of them. Differences are in the messages perceived, the healings documented, and their general importance for the world, but probably not so much in how they came about. It may be fair to assume that, similar to all genuine crop circles being formed by the same mechanism, all apparitions are likely coming about in generally the same way.

I see the mechanism of apparitional experiences as fundamentally very similar to how orbs, and by extension also crop circles, come about. They are also emanations from non-human intelligent Entities. The difference may primarily be that the apparitions of Fátima, Lourdes, and Medjugorje—and perhaps many other "Marian Apparitions"—may well be emanations from none other than the "Spirit Entity" Mother Mary herself.[72] It is then entirely conceivable that the apparitions come about as subtle energetic imprints, not on electronic charge plates like in the case of orbs, and not in biological tissue as in the case of crop circles, but in that which constitutes the energetic field where individual human awareness resides. It is known that brain waves of the type measured by scientists at the children in

---

[72] While there is no question in my mind that in the non-human consciousness arena there are no gender differences, there is likely still differentiation between masculine and feminine "principles." Mother Mary is the archetype of the feminine principle (nurturing, caring, loving), and as such using the feminine pronoun ("herself") seems definitely appropriate.

Medjugorje are energetically of the same order of magnitude (some 10^{-16} Ampere-seconds) with which orbs are imprinted on CCD charge plates in digital cameras.

It is noteworthy that the conscious entities emanating apparitions generally select children as their subjects to receive the apparitional experiences. This makes sense, given that children are more in tune with phenomena in general, less prone to mental bias, and less entrenched in conditioned beliefs, all of which would mean that they are more objective than grown people with well-established world views.

We can, therefore, logically conclude that, given the skill available in the realm of non-human intelligence, it is possible to energetically imprint distinct patterns in the mind of a person, just as easily as it would be to imprint orbs on a photographic charge plate, or affect kinking in grains in the making of a crop circle, or, as we will discuss in a subsequent chapter, make cell programming corrections in human tissue in the process which we call "spirit-directed healing."

PHENOMENOLOGICAL GIFTS

"Be true to purpose moment by moment. Cherish everything around you. The Light is always there, like a compass guiding your journey in life."
Akiane

There are many phenomena that people experience personally in their lives and that are so common that we often don't recognize them as phenomenological or even "unusual." We just take them for granted, perhaps as "gifts of talents." Surely, you might have met some of them in your own person.

For example, there is the gift of communicating in foreign languages. Most people have to study for years, they must diligently practice vocabulary, rehearse the most common phrases used in the language of their choice, acquire basic mastery of the grammar rules to finally become able to conduct a meaningful conversation in a foreign language. Our high school courses offered numerous language classes, and we took extensive advantage of them and spent years on mastering these desired communication skills. It always puzzles me when we meet people who claim to have "just picked it up," as they say. Our Brazilian taxi driver is one of them. Each year since we started using his services for airport transportation to and from our home in central Brazil, he seems to have expanded the topics in which he has become able to converse with us in English. He definitely belongs to the "eager learners," yet his ability to pick up new expressions seems quite remarkable and out of the ordinary. How many of these skills are gifted from the Field of Unlimited Possibilities to people, once they express an interest, we wondered.

There are other skills where this phenomenon of giftedness applies. Just think of the 18th century composer Wolfgang Amadeus Mozart. It is said that, as a preschooler, he listened to his older sister receiving piano lessons, before he was taught as well. In no time he was able to play beautiful sonatas, and soon after, at age six, he started composing magnificent music on his own. He composed his first symphony when he was just eight years old. Almost effortless, he became one of the greatest composers of all time. Music just seemed to come through, and he was called to express it. It is said that, as a young man, he traveled to Italy—certainly a long journey at the time—and, after he returned home, he made major compositions with tunes he heard on that travel, "just so." After years of piano lessons and practicing many hours to play some of his compositions, we are in awe about his creativity and the music gifts Mozart shared with the world during his short lifetime. Other composers, like Ludwig van Beethoven, Antonio Vivaldi, Georg Friedrich Händel, Johann Sebastian Bach, and many more, could be mentioned. They all showed clearly phenomenal skills in the mastery of music and seemed phenomenally chosen to inspire us with their gifts.

Shortly after we had published *The Orb Project* in 2007, we were, totally out of the blue, contacted by a film team from a TV network who wanted us to comment on a number of paintings by a young girl by the name of "Akiane." The paintings they showed us contained many circles, orb-like features, and they were wondering if these paintings were genuine representations of what the young artist (born in 1994) may have been seeing.[73] We had not heard about Akiane before, but were blown away to see her extraordinary paintings, which were most certainly indicative of much higher maturity than what would be expected of a child. We were very much aware that children are much more susceptible to intuitively acknowledging phenomena, such as orbs, than adults are who have been conditioned for many years to eliminate anything from their awareness that is not scientifically verifiable.[74] We later learned that Akiane started her love of painting at age 4 by skillfully sketching faces—with lots of orbs in them. Every year, her gallery of paintings expanded with

---

[73] To maintain neutrality, we are not mentioning the name of the TV Network.

[74] We interpreted these pictures as affirmatively showing what the young artist must have seen with her mind's eye—which was actually a response the skeptical lead reporter of the film team had not anticipated.

new themes and a versatility normally displayed only by the most experienced painters. For her, this form of expression seemed to flow onto the canvas with extreme speed and effortlessness. Akiane modestly quotes, "Be true to purpose moment by moment." She seems to acknowledge that her gift comes from somewhere else, and gratefully accepts it, as it brings her and others happiness. She also says, "Cherish everything around you; the Light is always there, like a compass guiding your journey in life."

There are numerous other examples of people receiving communications from an unknown origin to the extent that they develop incredible skills in one or the other fields, such as "Vitus," a 12-year old piano protégé, portrayed in a fascinating movie which friends gifted us a few years ago;[75] or people with savant syndrome, who may have significant mental disabilities in some areas but demonstrate certain other abilities far beyond average;[76] or many of the extraordinary scientists the world has seen over the centuries, such as Nostradamus, who predicted events centuries into the future, Michelangelo, or Leonardo da Vinci.

Could it be that people through whom extraordinary things manifest are especially in tune with the oneness of all that is, and are therefore chosen to receive phenomenal imprints in their mind to become extraordinary expressions of the miraculous, the beauty, and immense possibilities available to us? The examples we have given are certainly not ordinary gifts; they are, in fact, very much beyond what is the norm. But, on the other hand, could it not be argued that even much more mundane, day-by-day experienced "talents," which everyone of us exhibits—in various fields of what is recognized as "human expertise"—are really gifts conveyed upon us from the unseen Reality, from the Field of Unlimited Potential?

----

[75] See web reference: IMDb, "Vitus (2006)."

[76] The skills which savants often exhibit include photographic memory, speedy calculations, and alike.

We leave the reader with this question to ponder. Then we suggest to perhaps skip to Appendix (C)[77] of this book, where we describe a "scientific" experiment intended to obtain proof—once and for all—about certain characteristics of life on the "other side of Reality," which we also sometimes call the "Field of Unlimited Potential," but where we were instead given a very different, very unexpected, yet perfectly logical and immensely wise answer.

---

[77] This chapter in Appendix (C) is entitled *The Orb/EVP Experiment.* We placed it into the Appendix, because it falls a bit outside the scope of this book and was, in fact, reported—in an abbreviated version—in our earlier book *Expanding Perception.*

4.3 SOME THOUGHTS ABOUT THE
UFO PHENOMENON

"I happen to be privileged enough to be in on the fact that we have been visited on this planet, and the UFO phenomenon is real." **Edgar Mitchell**

In spite of the earlier mentioned miscue with the UFO/ET group in 2016—when a sudden intestinal problem made the decision for me to cancel my participation in a UFO symposium after I had second thoughts when it became clear to me that the emphasis of the symposium would be on UFO related government conspiracy and cover-up allegations—I have for decades been keenly interested in UFOs and related phenomena. At about the same time in 2016, Rey Hernandez, a phenomena researcher, contacted me. His work on non-human intelligence, performed within the *Dr. Edgar Mitchell Foundation for Research into Extraterrestrial and Extraordinary Experiences* (FREE), resonated much better with my own understanding. We are referring to this group later on in this chapter, when we share one of the most important conclusions about the UFO phenomenon.

The acronym "UFO" stands for "unidentified flying objects" and means many different things to different people, such as unidentified alien intelligence, nonhuman intelligence, flying saucers, spaceships, alien spacecraft, extraterrestrial vessel, etc. For the purpose of this chapter, we will classify all of these as UFO phenomena.

During the last 100 years, peaking in the 1940s and 50s, numerous sightings of unidentified flying objects were reported all over the world, predominantly in the United States. Many of the "experiencers" of these sightings did not perceive them as phenomena but as something very real, very tangible. Already quite early on, the US military saw in UFOs an existential threat to mankind coming from extraterrestrial beings. Under the pretense of not wanting to alarm the public, details about UFO and ET experiences were quickly swept under the rug, using various approaches to deflect public opinion away from the subject, such as intentional ridiculing those who would publicize or give credence to UFO/ET reports, and classifying UFO/ET sightings as secrets, thus making them inaccessible to the general public.

Now, decades later, these documents are beginning to become declassified, and the people who worked with them at the time, now mostly retired military personnel and scientists and engineers who worked in the military-industrial complex, are permitted to speak out about their experiences. One can find numerous such reports, and many hours of interviews with these people, on the Internet. Some of them are exceedingly interesting and poignant. But the effects of many decades of publicly ignoring and defaming anything that has to do with this topic are lingering, and the mainstream general public continues to be highly critical toward any notion of UFOs, ETs, and alike.

Meanwhile, it is all but impossible to even attempt to describe or summarize the wealth of information—and misinformation— about UFOs that is out in the public, or to give any sort of scholarly review of this phenomenon. We will refrain from doing this and refer the reader to the Internet and, in particular, the excellent book by Hernandez, Klimo, and Schild.[78] Instead, we will describe those aspects of the UFO experience that we consider relevant for the ensuing discussion. This is going to be biased. A number of people who have seen or heard about UFOs and/or ETs may disagree with one or the other point we are making.

---

[78] A scholarly book about this topic has recently been published by Rey Hernandez, Jon Klimo, and Rudy Schild of the Dr. Edgar Mitchell FREE Foundation, titled *Beyond UFOs: The Science of Consciousness and Contact with Non-Human Intelligence.*

DEFINITIONS, CONTEXT, AND
BOUNDARIES OF THIS DISCUSSION

Given the massive amount of information and misinformation available about UFOs in the public domain, we must attempt to untangle science from science fiction to expand our insights from this important phenomenon.

From the wealth of what is known about UFOs, I will now list those details that seem particularly interesting to me: [79]

(1) By and large, UFOs have been sighted from considerable distance, and they were seen and/or photographed in low resolution, i.e., their contours were not sharp or crisp. In photos, they appear out of focus, colorless, often simply as small undefined blobs, "resembling" the shape of saucers or imaginary spaceships, or alike.[80]

(2) While the U.S. government, as well as other foreign governments, predominantly perceived UFOs as threatening to humanity, we notice that an overwhelming number of actual UFO experiencers, i.e., of those people who have

---

[79] I am intentionally steering away from citing and dealing with the wealth of "academic" information about the subject, such as the *Drake Equation* (elaborated in a subsequent footnote), and the *Fermi Paradox* (where I agree with the basic tenet that many earth-like planets must be assumed to exist in the universe but disagree that there is a paradox, i.e., where I question the supposition that we should by now have physical evidence thereof). I am also not engaging in the multitude of attempts by many profiled researchers to explain the "Fermi Paradox" (which is well summarized in https://en.wikipedia.org/wiki/Fermi_paradox). Instead, I prefer not to contribute to that discussion at this point but to emphasize the conclusions drawn in the present context.

[80] I realize that there are numerous UFO experiencers and researchers who do not agree with this generalization and insist that they have seen—or have heard from people who have seen—UFOs in close proximity and with sharp, materialistic looking features. Consider these to be exceptions which we will deal with separately.

seen and reported personally about a UFO encounter, had a positive, uplifting, enriching experience about them.

(3) Some reports show UFO-type vessels and machinery from close distance and in good image resolution. In view of (5) below, I have reservations that these are, in fact, genuine UFO sightings.

(4) We have ourselves observed what credible people studying UFOs ("ufologists") would call UFO-type "spaceships." These sightings were from a significant distance, perhaps several miles afar, during night hours, far away from any city lights. They looked very much like distant commercial aircraft, with the exception that they had no blinking but weak steady lights, and their flight trajectories, albeit generally straight, would at times unexpectedly and abruptly change by as much as 90 degrees.[81] They were so far away that they essentially appeared as tiny moving dots in the sky, not at all different from how distant aircraft appear under low-lighting conditions in the night sky, but due to the evidential abrupt change of flight direction they were clearly "unusual."

(5) Following reports about recently declassified UFO related information,[82] the US government has, over several decades, spent many millions of dollars toward efforts to cover up what they know about UFO technology. This was done even to the extent that they contracted the top secret manufacturing of UFO-look-alike aircraft that were designed and manufactured for the primary, or even sole, purpose of demonstrating to the public, by deliberate information leakage, something that would suggest that UFOs are "fake and really do not exist," and that it is "unfashionable" to still believe in UFOs.

---

[81] These observations occurred on May 23, 2014, at *Eceti Ranch* in Trout Lake, WA, at the foot of Mt. Adams, on the property of famed ufologist James Gilliland. They were witnessed by a group of about 20 seminar participants, including Gundi and myself.

[82] Dr. Stephen Greer (e.g., in *The Disclosure Project*), and others.

PROBABILITY REGARDING LIFE IN
THE MILKY WAY GALAXY

An estimate of a 0.01% probability that there is highly intelligent life anywhere else in our galaxy at this time may be a conservative approximation.

We are now making a series of assumptions that are all, by their nature, unsubstantiated—because conclusive better answers are not yet available—but, in aggregate, may not be all that terribly wrong. They all pertain to our physical universe, i.e., they do not take into consideration the concept, or potential existence, of parallel universes, with which we deal in a subsequent chapter.

A. Our Milky Way galaxy has about 100 billion (10^{11}) stars and perhaps an equal number of planets (probably more, but let's, for reasons of simplicity, use this number).

B. If we assume that, at some point in time between the Big Bang and now, every millionth of these planets evolved some sort of biological life, this would mean that 100,000 planets in the Milky Way may have, or may have had at some point in time, biological life on them.

C. Let us assume that 1% of these, or 1000, developed into conscious civilizations with technological capabilities similar to what humankind has achieved.

D. Let us conservatively consider that each of these 1000 civilizations may have succeeded in the technological capability of interstellar travel for a period of 1000 years, after which it is/was extinguished due to self-destruction or some other fatal cataclysmic event.

E. We further assume that these intelligent civilizations have occurred ("lived") randomly during the last ten billion of the thirteen billion years of the life span of the galaxy.

With these assumptions, each of which cannot be scientifically substantiated, we come to a combined total period of one million years (1000 civilizations*1000 years each), during which the Milky Way Galaxy may have had a civilization that was potentially capable of interstellar travel. This is only 1/10,000[th] of the last 10 billion years of the life span of the Galaxy (1 million/10 billion = 10^{-4}). Therefore, even if each one of these 1000 civilizations had developed the technology to travel to any place in the galaxy, the probability of finding another civilization contemporaneously at the peak of its technological evolution[83] is only 1 in 10,000, or 0.01%. Or, in other words, with 99.99% probability there are at this time no other intelligent life forms anywhere in the Galaxy with which we could attempt to make contact, even if we or they were capable of interstellar travel at unlimited speeds, i.e., so fast that we could reach anywhere within the galaxy in relatively short time.[84]

---

[83] Again, it is important to emphasize that we are talking about technological evolution, not the evolution of a biological species. On Earth, for example, we had an advanced evolution of the "dinosaur" biological species several tens of millions of years ago, but it was not technologically advanced.

[84] This is, in part, a simplification of the "Drake Equation" (Frank Drake, 1961— https://www.space.com/25219-drake-equation.html):

$$N = R_* * f_p * n_e * f_l * f_i * f_c * L$$

Where:

N = The number of civilizations in the Milky Way Galaxy whose electromagnetic emissions are detectable.
R_* = The rate of formation of stars suitable for the development of intelligent life.
f_p = The fraction of those stars with planetary systems.
n_e = The number of planets, per solar system, with an environment suitable for life.
f_l = The fraction of suitable planets on which life actually appears.
f_i = The fraction of life bearing planets on which intelligent life emerges.
f_c = The fraction of civilizations that develop a technology that releases detectable signs of their existence into space.
L = The length of time such civilizations release detectable signals into space.

Before we continue, let us look at the reasonableness of our assumptions and, perhaps, consider some upper and lower limit variations. The biggest unknown factor is likely a combination of assumptions B. and C. One might argue that there are more than 1000 planets in our Galaxy that had, at some point in time, civilizations capable of interstellar travel. One might even argue that this number is off by as much as a factor 1000, i.e., that there were 1 million such planets. However, by the same token argument, the duration during which this capability persisted before these civilizations became extinct may have averaged more likely 100 than 1000 years. This combined adjustment of our assumptions would reduce the probability that at least one such civilization anywhere in the Milky Way coincides with humankind at this time from 0.01% to about 1%. On the other hand, one might say that there are, or were, many fewer planets with significant civilizations, perhaps only 100. In fact, there are modern schools of research—albeit equally unsubstantiated— stating that this number may be more likely in the single digits. This would then further decrease the probability of overlap in time.

We therefore think that, for the purpose of the ensuing discussion, our earlier presented estimate of 0.01% probability that there is highly intelligent life anywhere else in our galaxy at this moment in cosmic time may be a conservative approximation.

PROBABILITY OF PHYSICAL UFO
CONTACT WITHIN OUR GALAXY

The possibility of ever meeting-up with biological/physical life existing concurrently with us in our galaxy, at this very time in the history of the universe, is so unrealistic that winning big in the lottery would be about a thousand times more probable.

This low probability of finding contemporaneous life in our Galaxy is further very significantly reduced by the realism of interstellar travel. We do realize, however, that many futurists make the blunt assumption that somehow, given enough time for technological development, it will be possible to devise the technology with which physical objects (i.e., biological/physical beings containing physical mass) can travel faster than the speed of light. In fact, they would have to travel not just a bit faster, but by many orders of magnitude faster than the speed of light, to reach destinations anywhere within the Galaxy within some reasonably short time. Some futurists would even state that the probability of reaching this degree of technological perfection "must surely be" very high. We disagree.

Another school of thinking postulates that other planets with highly evolved civilizations may exist that are invisible and therefore heretofore undetected, because they may be subject to different laws of physics. They could, so the thinking, be built around different "mass densities," and the physics for those systems could be conceived of as being so different that the fastest permissible velocities in those systems could be substantially higher than the speed of light. Such planets, they argue, could be close to Earth, within reasonable travel distance, considering the potentiality that the evolution of their civilizations might be so advanced that travel at their much higher equivalent "Speed of light" might be possible.

Such arguments are difficult for me; they might fall in the category of parallel universes which we discuss in a subsequent chapter. For the purpose of relevancy for the discussion in this chapter, which deals with probabilities related to our physical universe, I will discard the possibility of existence of such lower density—yet still physical—planets with presumably highly intelligent life forms.[85] Intelligent physical life, as I am assuming as basis for our thought experiment, is tied to essentially known physics and physical mass, which to move in any way at speeds many orders of magnitude greater than the speed of light is impossible.[86]

The reader may note that our disregard of the potential existence of lower density planets and life forms is only significant in the framework of this book as it relates to maximum process speeds. Even if such invisible lower density planets and biological life forms were to exist, they would be subject to some other set of laws of physics; and unless the maximum speed permissible under these other laws would be several orders of magnitude greater than our (conventional) speed of light (300,000 km/s), they would have to be discarded and could not be considered feasible within the framework of the following discussion.

Getting back to galaxies, planets, and evolved physical/biological beings that are subject to our conventional understanding of physics, we find that even getting anywhere near the speed of light (300,000 km/s) will be excruciatingly difficult. But we will, for the sake of this argument, concede that it may be possible; i.e., we will assume that people may at some point in time be able to travel as fast as close to the speed of light, but certainly not faster than that.

---

[85] I am emphasizing that I relate this statement to physical objects or beings that contain physical mass, not to nonphysical beings of any kind that do not contain physical mass. It is very important to acknowledge this distinction for this train of thought.

[86] I am deliberately phrasing it this way to circumvent arguments that it has been proven that some physical processes (involving minute amounts of physical mass) can move at speeds a bit faster than the speed of light, but not many orders of magnitude faster.

Furthermore, we then assume that no intelligent being, human or alien, will realistically want to undertake a space travel taking more than, say, ten years to get to an intended destination. The nearest planet outside the solar system is about 4.5 lightyears away from us, and the average distance between stars in our galaxy is about 5 lightyears. Consequently, the number of planets outside our solar system that we could conceivably reach with interstellar travel at the speed of light is extremely limited, certainly less than, say, ten.[87]

We argued earlier that as many as about a thousand planets in our galaxy may conceivably have evolved technologically highly advanced civilizations capable of space travel at the speed of light at some time during the 13.5 billion-year existence of the galaxy. The probability that any one of them happens to be among the ten planets that are within about ten lightyears from to our solar system is then one in ten million ($10*1000/100,000,000,000$, or about 10^{-7}). If we, furthermore, multiply this with the earlier derived probability (10^{-4}) that this star happens to have this technological capability concurrently with us— at this very time in the history of the universe—we come to a total probability to ever meet up with other conscious life in our Galaxy of about 10^{-11}, or somewhere around a millionth of one percent. This is a very low probability, indeed. Winning big in the lottery would be about a thousand times more probable[88] than that.

Let's add a few words with regard to the accuracy of such "back-on-the-envelope" considerations. A few decades ago, my esteemed Ph.D. thesis advisor, Applied Physics Professor Dr. G. Möllenstedt of the University of Tübingen, Germany, who was then also head of the university's reputable Department of Astronomy, phrased in his lectures the wise statement, "There is nothing that signifies the ineptitude of a physicist or an astronomer more than calculating with

---

[87] Much more realistically, we would have to call this probability zero, but we do not have to commit to this extreme for the purposes of what we are trying to establish here.

[88] Mathematically, the probability of winning the Powerball Lottery is about 1 in 175 million (10^{-8}), which is about 1000 times higher than 10^{-11}.

excessive numerical accuracy." In our case, more accuracy would be irrelevant for the purpose of this discussion—it would not change the fact that, for all practical purposes, humanity will never be able to meet up, and communicate with, physical life from other planets or stars in this universe. This is simply impossible. End of argument!

I should then emphasize that this statement is limited to direct bilateral communication, such as physically meeting with ET-type intelligent beings, or directly seeing them in their natural environment, or their "spaceship," and bilaterally interacting with them. The probability of intercepting signals coming from other planets in our Galaxy that are, or were at some point in time, home to intelligent life is, of course, much higher. Such signals would be of the type of electromagnetic waves, traveling at the speed of light. They would be very faint, due to decay during very long "travel" through space and high dispersion—not deliberately focused toward Earth. They could be detected with large parabolic antennas designed for this purpose, even after millions of years of travel. Such information could then be coming from very far away, from deep within the Galaxy, and not just from the few planets that are closest to the solar system. But of course, this would just be an academically interesting one-directional receipt of some sort of information indicating the existence of intelligent life somewhere else in the Galaxy, likely long in the past. We might even be able to pinpoint from which star or planet—or at least from which general location within the Galaxy—it originated, but due to the long travel times involved, it would of course be impossible to respond and thus bilaterally communicate with that life form.

Therefore, if we translate this finding to the topic of UFOs, we can, for all practical purposes, eliminate that there are physical spaceships of any imaginable kind that they carry any "extra-terrestrial physical beings" of any kind from any planet from anywhere in our galaxy.

But what then are UFOs? If there are no physical ETs, no physical UFOs that could ever visit us, what is it that multitudes of people over the decades have been seeing and convincingly reporting about? Before we entertain this very important question, let us take a quick and cursory look at the probability of contemporaneous existence of conscious life elsewhere in the physical universe, outside of the Milky Way galaxy.

PROBABILITY OF LIFE ELSEWHERE
IN THE PHYSICAL UNIVERSE

There is an overwhelmingly high probability that many highly evolved civilizations exist elsewhere in the physical Universe, even contemporaneously with us, but the Grand Original Design provides that there is a zero chance to ever physically meet and exchange notes with any one of them.

We are asking what the chances would be for physical/biological life to exist, at this very point in cosmic time, anywhere else in the physical universe. How probable might it be that there are other planets in the universe that happen to have similar conditions to Earth that are favorable for the evolution of physical/biological life of some sort, to the extent that such life forms evolved to a technological advancement similar to, or even greater than that on Earth.

Again, with this question I am explicitly addressing physical beings, like we assume ETs to be, who would have physical mass and would physically live on some sort of planet, subject to gravity, and require vehicles to move from place to place on that planet and perhaps into its spatial vicinity. I am specifically not including intelligent beings that have no physicality, such as those that we would describe as spirit or angelic beings.

It is estimated that there are about a hundred billion (10^{11}) galaxies in the universe.[89] I don't think that there is any pertinent information available that would justify an assumption that the probability of conscious life in these other galaxies is any different than what it is in the Milky Way galaxy. So, it can be considered reasonable to assume that we have a hundred billion times a situation that is similar to that

---

[89] Some futurists, including Dr. Deepak Chopra, believe that this estimate may be low by several orders of magnitude. Nobody really knows, and for the purposes of what we want to communicate here, our low number is perfectly sufficient.

of our own galaxy. This would translate to a clear prognosis that it is extremely likely that somewhere in the universe there is an intelligent civilization at this very time, i.e., overlapping in galactic time with humanity, that would be capable of some sort of space travel. The probability for that to happen concurrently with humanity in the Milky Way galaxy is, as we stated, very low (of the order of 0.01%), but given the huge number of other galaxies we have to contend with, we come up with a likelihood that not only one, but actually a very significant number of evolved civilizations, like humanity, exist at this very time somewhere in the universe. We are simply multiplying a small probability (10^{-4}) of temporally overlapping civilizations for one galaxy (Milky Way) with a very large number of galaxies existing in total in the physical universe (10^{11}) to come up with a large number of civilizations (with our assumptions about 10 million) that can be assumed to exist at this specific cosmic time in the entire universe. Additionally, several orders of magnitude more such civilizations have likely existed at some other point in time in the universe but have long since become extinct.

However, travelling to or from there, and meeting up with such conscious concomitantly living physical beings, is totally and completely beyond any probability—unless someone wants to spend upwards of 2.5 million years to get there while traveling at the speed of light, because this is the number of light years by which just the nearest neighboring galaxy, the Andromeda galaxy, is separated from us. Therefore, the probability that we would ever meet any spaceship or ET or have any other form of intelligent information exchange from/with beings from another galaxy in this Universe is "zero"—not 10^{-11}, which we crudely calculated for the case from within our own galaxy, but it is for all practical purposes zero. Again, this is based on the assumption that it will never be possible for a physical entity of any kind[90] to travel at speeds that are by many orders of magnitude faster than the speed of light.

---

[90] Let us make clear what we mean when we talk about a physical entity, or about physicality as opposed to non-physicality. The decisive distinction is mass. Physicality contains mass, or matter, non-physicality does not.

Any argumentation to the contrary, i.e., any proposition by people that they have witnessed physical UFOs and/or ETs, would have to refute this assumption, i.e., would have to include the untenable implication that these UFOs and/or ETs were able to travel at speeds not just a bit faster, but by many orders of magnitude faster than the speed of light. "Beaming" people and equipment from one place in the physical universe to another may be possible in the minds of futurists and filmmakers, but likely not in real "reality."

Let us stay with the ramifications of this conclusion a bit longer. We have established that it will essentially never (with a probability of about 10^{-11}) be possible for our civilization to have bilateral physical encounters with a civilization outside of our planet. But, on the other hand, there is an overwhelmingly high probability that many such highly evolved civilizations do exist elsewhere in this Universe—we have just no chance of ever meeting up with any of them. Existence and being able to make physical contact are two very different propositions. The former is essentially certain, the latter is essentially impossible.[91]

Therefore, a conclusion that homo sapiens might be the only species capable of evolving that, which God is, would be highly presumptuous. The physical universe appears to be designed in such a superb way that any evolution of consciousness, in any thinkable and unthinkable direction, is by design. The grandeur of this **G**rand **O**riginal **D**esign, which is underlying the creation of the entire physical universe, is indeed unfathomable. It involves not only humanity but countless other conscious civilizations anywhere in our galaxy and the universe at large. But the Design includes that one will never meet with the other. This is AWE-some.

---

[91] As a caveat we point to a subsequent chapter (entitled *Is the UFO Phenomenon Related to a Parallel Universe?*), where we entertain the hypothetical question if UFOs and ETs might possibly come not from this universe but from a parallel universe. From what we know now, such a proposition is science fiction—based on a notion which I find scientifically untenable that we "must surely find" a better explanation for ETs and UFOs than categorizing them as nonphysical phenomena.

UFO AS NONPHYSICAL PHENOMENON

UFO and ET-related reports must be re-interpreted. It is not feasible that people can be physically picked up by a "spaceship," taken to another planet or just kept on the spaceship for some physical time and perhaps some health-related procedure, and then be redelivered into our terrestrial physical reality. We are not stating that such reports are unsubstantiated, but we argue that they most likely are misinterpretations. They are phenomenological, not physical, even when the end result of such an experience is of a verifiable physical nature. They involve nonphysical aspects of human existence.

Prior to my realization that it is statistically impossible to be visited by physical beings from a different world within our physical universe, as I described above, I had tentatively divided UFO experiences in two categories, physical and phenomenological. What experiencers very often believe ETs to be would fit in the first of these categories, i.e., that they are of a physical nature. Now that this must be taken out of consideration, it appears that the only reasonable conclusion left to be taken seriously is that UFOs and ETs are nonphysical phenomena.[92]

It is, then, not farfetched to compare the UFO phenomenon with the Orb phenomenon, which we have studied extensively for many years. There are several interesting commonalities and differences. Orbs in photos are relatively small and often not well-defined in their contours—as are UFOs. But sometimes, orbs have non-circular outer contours,[93] or very intricate interiorities, for example human-like

---

[92] This is a striking conclusion; one that will certainly be at odds with many ufologists all over the world.

[93] One usually sees orbs from the front, as if it is "looking at you." But we have also seen them from the side, as shown in the rare photo below in this footnote (*Photo 11*), where—due to mirroring effects—the camera "happened to" see the orb from the side. The similarity to some sort of "flying saucer" is astonishing. Note that the photo on the left shows the arrangement: we are inside a room; the

faces. We have described this in detail in *Orbs, Their Mission and Messages of Hope*.[94] Similarly, UFO sightings sometimes include remarkable visual details about the nonhuman "flying" object that was observed. However, while faces or interiorities inside orbs can be quite intricate, they are not at all as clear as photographs of real physical objects. The same holds true for photos of typical UFO sightings.

Perhaps one major difference between orbs and UFO phenomena is that spirit orbs are not normally visible with the human eye. They are detectable predominantly only on photo or video recordings. Only very few people can actually visually see them. We present examples in our book *Orbs, Their Mission and Messages of Hope*. It appears to be the other way around with UFO phenomena; they were at first—perceived as—seen with the human eye and then recorded with cameras.

---

photographer is looking at some sort of desk or dresser containing a mirror which creates a reflection of the flash, and the orb—in the top left corner of the photo—is "looking" at the flash coming from that mirror and not, as would usually be the case, directly into the camera flash. The right photo shows this orb cropped and strongly magnified.

Photo 11: Orb serendipitously photographed from the side: it is oriented toward a mirror, located on the dresser, which reflected the flash in the top left corner of the room; right: magnified orb (photo courtesy of Christine Coveney, 2011).

[94] See also the chapter entitled *Interiorities of Orbs*, where we show an orb in diamond shape.

Orbs carry messages from the unseen, non-physical reality; and so do, by inference, UFOs. These messages are very real and often personal. They communicate that there is a much larger "real" reality than what we currently experience based on our very limited frame of reference of the physical reality. Most importantly, that invisible reality is benevolent to humankind and its evolutionary development.

From our orbs research we have learned that the nonphysical entities communicating these messages make use of our own physical technical achievements. They would make every effort to appear in such a way that they are most readily noticed. In the case of orbs, these technical achievements have been highly energy-sensitive photographic recording devices that are in the common domain, available to multitudes of people at relatively low cost. The little opaque orb circles became clearly noticeable. They are undeniable. The shape of the orbs, so we learned, is generally in accordance with what would most readily attract the attention of those for whom the orb messages are intended—orbs with faces, orbs with different outer shapes, orbs in colors, etc.

Before digital cameras were mass-marketed in the early years of the 21st century, spirit orbs were practically unknown, and the nonphysical entities used other, then available technological achievements that would lend themselves for producing attention grabbing and energetically feasible phenomena. Since the 1930s, aircraft were such a fascinating technological development. We have seen orbs during bright daylight. Hence it is not surprising that "orbs in the shape of flying objects" were designed by the nonphysical beings in the unseen reality to get people's attention at that time. They needed to be visible in daylight, noticeable with the bare eye, and persist long enough that they could be photographed or filmed with the analog photographical equipment available at the time.

These "apparition"-like UFO phenomena would certainly require more energy to "manufacture" than what is nowadays required for recording of orbs on highly sensitive CCD-camera charge plates, but it is unquestionably energetically possible for beings in that realm—we know this from recordings of high-resolution orbs with regular, much less sensitive emulsion film cameras.[95] It is perhaps a bit more difficult than recording "standard" orbs, which may explain why UFOs are, and were, observed far less frequently than orbs are seen nowadays.

Our conclusion that physical UFOs and ETs can likely not exist means that many UFO and ET-related reports by experiencers, including reports of "abductions," need to be re-interpreted. It is very unlikely that people can be physically picked up by a "spaceship" that originated from another planet somewhere in the universe, taken to another planet or just kept on the spaceship for some physical time, and then be re-delivered into our terrestrial physical reality. We are not stating that such reports are unsubstantiated, but they appear misinterpreted. These reported events are likely phenomenological, not physical. They involve nonphysical aspects of human existence. The physicality of the experiencers is not involved. The physical bodies of the experiencers remain exactly where they happen to be before the completely nonphysical encounter with beings from the nonphysical reality starts.[96]

What is the relevance of all of this? It's huge:

■ It conveys that we, humanity at large, are on our own. While there are very likely many other intelligent civilizations in other galaxies, even now, at the very time during which our own, terrestrial civilization—*homo sapiens*—is peaking, physical contact with any one of them is, for all practical purposes, impossible. We will not have to fear being taken

---

[95] See the work of the Dutch professional photographer Ed Vos, who photographed many beautiful, large orbs with his professional emulsion film analog photo-cameras.

[96] This is, for example, corroborated in numerous credible near-death experiences (NDEs), where the experiencers reported having seen their own physicality from afar, such as lying on the operating table and being operated on by "physicians."

over by creatures from another world. All we have to deal with are belligerent adversaries from within our own planet, but not from other planets in our galaxy or the physical universe. Our problems, big enough as they are, are limited, a known quantity. There are no unknown monsters out there that might attack us, take away what we have – the enemy is us, among our own species.

- It reveals that, whatever we sometimes seem to see that looks like having "extraterrestrial" origin, is not a physical object or biological sentient being from a far-away planet in our galaxy or any other galaxy, but it is rather a nonphysical, phenomenological experience.

- It communicates that there is a reality out there that is nonphysical and has no spatial or temporal boundaries and includes highly evolved conscious nonphysical beings that are benevolent toward humanity. They want to help us in all situations of life but need, on an individual basis, our concurrence to let them do so. They want to communicate this to us and try out every possible way to get our attention for this to happen, which is difficult, given our general human state of hubris.

- It tells that these nonphysical beings do have energetics at their avail. These energies are many orders of magnitude weaker than "regular" physical energies. We sometimes call them "subtle energies." They are sufficient in magnitude to imprint patterns in human minds or on biological matter, as we will discuss later, and they are sufficient to imprint information onto highly sensitive hi-tech sensors, such as CCD charge plates in digital cameras that approach single-photon recording sensitivity.

- It imparts a feeling of humility, in that we learn that humanity is not the only cognitive species in the universe, but there may well be, and have been throughout the history of the physical universe, very many, perhaps billions of other highly evolved civilizations somewhere out there that have similar development potential than that granted to humanity. They are all part of the **_Grand Original Design_**; or, depending on one's religious persuasion, one might say that they are all God's creation.

We are picking up this discussion in a subsequent chapter in which we draw conclusions from a large variety of phenomena, including also crop circles, apparitions, and spirit-directed healing. We do, however, first wish to say a few words about the notion of "parallel universes." Might UFO and ET phenomena possibly be related to a parallel universe?

IS THE UFO PHENOMENON RELATED
TO A PARALLEL UNIVERSE?

It is theoretically not entirely inconceivable that a parallel universe may exist and has a sun and planets similar to ours and shares in our own universal space and is locally intertwined with our solar system. Communication with highly evolved sentient beings from a parallel universe would then not be subject to the speed of light limitations that render meet-ups between civilizations within the "regular" physical universe impossible.

During the past few years I have—often with consternation—observed the political divide in the United States. Like never before, there seem to be two irreconcilable factions: those who support the Administration and those who oppose it. It feels like there is no gray area in-between these factions; nobody appears to be on neutral grounds. It's either one or the other. It is as if we are split in two different worlds. The word "bipartisan" seems to have been all but eradicated from the vocabulary.

In a way, the same sensation holds when we go outside of politics to other aspects of life. Take religious belief systems. Radical Islamists, fundamentalist Christians, orthodox Jews, each seem to be living in their own universe. And then there are New Age spiritualists, extreme environmentalists, and so on – one can add to this list *ad libitum*. When one looks at the extremism represented in each of these factions, one might facetiously say that they are living in a "parallel universe." Of course, we know that this is a facetious expression. But is there more to this concept?

Let us recall that, so far in this book, we have deliberately limited our discussion to the physical universe. We have categorically stated that, within the physical universe—which is so immense that we cannot even begin to fathom its size, stretching over thirteen billion light years and comprising some hundred billion galaxies, each of which with some hundred billion stars and planets—there is no possibility that civilizations living on different planets will ever be able to physically meet up with each other. Physics tells us that it is impossible. Is that the end of the story?

For physicists, the Einsteinian Age has brought a certain advanced understanding of our physical universe. We are beginning to take theories of the beginnings, evolution, expansion of the Universe, for granted. Humanity is in the beginning of undertaking space travel and understands its requirements and limitations imposed by the speed of light; we know how tiny a fraction of the vastness of space we might actually ever be able to penetrate. We have a conceptual understanding of what black holes[97] are. We are grasping the impact of Quantum theory. We have learned an enormous amount about the microcosm and the macrocosm. We know, for example, that the Universe is not a vacuum but that it is interspersed with the equivalent of as much as one hydrogen atom per cubic centimeter of space; and we know that, on the other hand, the entire universe, with all its galaxies, stars and planets, is essentially one endless volume of "empty" space, and you and I and all physical matter around us consists of nothing but an agglomeration of super-tiny nuclei suspended in an endless vacuum. And we understand that everything that exists in this universe obeys a set of basic laws of physics that

---

[97] Black Holes can be understood as collapsed, burnt-out stars. When insufficient energy is left to keep the charge density alive that maintains the distance between atoms, the gravitational forces of the atomic nuclei can become predominant, and the "house of cards" of the atoms collapses, reducing the volume of individual atoms to the much, much smaller volume of the actual atomic nuclei. Due to the collapse to a much smaller volume, the undiminished gravitational forces, which are inversely proportional to the square of the distance from the center of mass of the nuclei, increase and cause more atoms to collapse. Once started, the process progresses with extreme speed. Everything that is anywhere near is sucked up by the ever-increasing gravity of the growing black hole. Within a fraction of a moment, the entire dying star ends up being converted to the mass of the black hole. The gravitational force near the center of the black hole becomes so huge that everything, even light, is pulled into it and cannot escape. Something from which nothing can emerge is black—hence the descriptive name "black hole."

are built upon very few physical nature constants with interstellar validity. The speed of light is one of them.

In recent years, some physicists have begun to venture into theorems that go even beyond this unimaginably huge physical universe. They argue that it is conceivable that there is not just one universe, as unfathomably big as it is, but that there may be other universes, each of which can conceivably be built entirely differently. They can be understood as having originated in different "Big Bang"-type cataclysmic events, or have unimaginable other origins, resulting in entirely different sets of laws of physics, and they could thus exist entirely separate and undetectable from each other.

Most importantly, given that our own universe exists in essentially entirely empty space, it would be conceivable that another universe, or even a multitude of other universes, exists that shares in our own "universal space." It is, therefore, not inconceivable that a parallel universe exists that has a sun and planets just like ours, and that is locally intertwined with our solar system. It could have different building blocks (different atoms or atomic structures), different long-range and short-range forces, different sets of laws of physics, etc., all so different that we would likely not even be able to detect its presence.

All this is conceivable, but we have so far not been able to prove any of this, because there is no understandable physical mechanism by which a parallel universe could be understood as being interconnected with our physical universe.

There are, on the other hand, unconventional and unsubstantiated arguments that there may be such a thing as "a back side" of a "Black Hole," that this might be what would connect to a parallel universe. There are certain phenomena that can be interpreted in favor of such an argument. None of them is, at least up to this point in time, anything more than wild speculation. But then, even such a speculation is interesting. We want to mention three seemingly unrelated "observations" that hint at a possibility that the concept of existence of a parallel universe may be more real at second thought than at first.

One observation of a physically recorded phenomenon hinting in this direction is orb photography by Dr. Miceal Ledwith, first published in 2007 in our joint book *"The Orb Project,"* where a torsion effect of orbs seems to be visible in a series of orb photos. A multitude of orbs appears positioned at the entrance to what looks like a funnel, whereby the orbs in the center of the funnel opening appear radially distorted.[98] Could this signify the horrendous gravitational field expected to exist at the entrance of a black hole? Could this be evidence for interconnection between our reality and a parallel universe? Are black holes passage ways for transitioning from one to another universe? Nobody knows; there are too many unanswered questions—but the thought is intriguing.

Other examples for a possible existence of a parallel universe are phenomenological life experiences of a number of people, as reported by Hernandez *et al.* in their 2018 book *The Science of Consciousness and Contact with Non-Human Intelligence.* Various "experiencers" have credibly reported otherworldly encounters, such as abductions, with beings and equipment that they perceived as "real" and "materialistic," i.e., consisting of "real" biological and physical matter, rather than as non-material phenomena. Since we must exclude, for reasons of prohibitive travel times, as we explained in the previous chapters, that these might have been encounters with material/biological beings from elsewhere within our physical universe, the concept of a parallel universe, where travel times are not prohibitive, lends itself as a fallback hypothetical explanation. I must, however, emphasize that our earlier interpretation that all

---

[98] The book *"The Orb Project"* came about as a combination of two manuscripts of pioneering research on orbs. The publisher had received two manuscripts, one by Dr. Ledwith and one by myself, that were looking at orbs in different ways. We both, as well as the author of the foreword, professor Dr. William Tiller, came to the conclusion that orbs are not of this world. The photos showing torsion effects (in particular I-36 to I-41) came from Dr. Ledwith's manuscript, and he deserves all credit for these photos.

these experiences, no matter how realistic they may have been for the experiencer, are of a phenomenological nature continues to be more compelling to me.[99]

There are also teachings of certain spiritually oriented groups that can be interpreted as describing a civilization in a parallel universe. One such group is the world-wide *Spiritist Movement* which dates back to the mid 19th century and was spearheaded by the French scientist, teacher and philosopher *Léon Denizard Rivail*, who became known under the pseudo-name *Allan Kardec* (1804 - 1869). The most prolific semi-contemporary author representing this movement is the Brazilian *Francisco (Chico) Xavier* (1910 - 2002).[100] He wrote over 450 books, all of which were channeled by various discarnate spirit entities. Arguably his most famous book is titled *Nosso Lar,* which was "dictated" (channeled) in 1943 by a spirit entity identified as *André Luiz.* It describes the afterlife of a medical doctor as if it were taking place in an environment very similar to a terrestrial setting. It is my personal impression that this book is a description of the afterlife through the eyes and imagination of a specific spirit entity (André Luiz), adapted to the frame of mind of the majority of the readers at that time. However, I cannot entirely exclude the possibility that the circumstances of the afterlife world, as described in *Nosso Lar,* may, in fact, give a fairly factual description of life on a "planet" similar to earth, in a parallel universe.

The topic of parallel universes is certainly intriguing, but it is also highly speculative. It is beyond the scope of this book to even begin to discuss this subject outside of the narrow context within which it surfaced, which is its relevance to phenomena in general and to the UFO and ET phenomenon in particular. Relevance in this

---

[99] Remember, for example from Chapter 4.2, that the experiencers in Medjugorje, or Fátima or Lourdes, stated with persistence that what they saw was the "real" Holy Mother appearing to them.

[100] Chico Xavier is recognized as one of the most productive mediums and inspirational writers of all time. There has been overwhelming witness corroboration that he wrote his "psychographic" books in a channeling mode.

context has to do with physicality, i.e., whether or not physical mass is involved. Even in an entirely different physical reality, such as a parallel universe, something like physical mass must be assumed to exist, and it must then be concluded that a maximum permissible speed of travel exists. It may not be the same as it is in our physical reality (i.e., not necessarily 300,000 km/sec), but it would likely be confining as far as travel from one planet to another within that parallel universe is concerned, similar to how the speed of light impacts interstellar travel in our universe.

However, if parallel universes are more than utopia, the assumption that different universes will occupy the same space is probably realistic. This would then mean that planets with conscious life in two different universes could in principle be spatially located very close to each other. Travel between one and the other might then conceivably be possible without the constraints of huge travel times, *if* a "technology" were to exist to transition from one to the other universe, i.e., from one to the other set of underlying physics.

Keeping our feet a bit more on solid grounds, in this book we describe that intelligent beings in the "Reality Beyond"—whatever this may mean for different people—are capable of impressing us with phenomenological experiences that can seem so real that the recipients of these phenomena interpret them in certain ways that make them most plausible to them. In our understanding, this Reality Beyond is not a part of our physical Universe, and it is also not part of a parallel universe which, by definition, also has physicality—albeit of a different kind. The Reality Beyond is truly non-physical, in that it has no physical mass.

Confused? Consider the following simplified summary. We are dealing with two realities, the physical reality and the nonphysical or spiritual reality. The latter is characterized by absence of physical mass. The physical reality includes everything that has mass, i.e., it includes every "thing" in our universe and every "thing" in parallel universes, if they exist.

Phenomena originate in the nonphysical reality. They are not of this world, i.e., they are not of this universe, and they are not of a parallel universe. They are of energetic origin and affect us energetically.

4.4 HEALING PHENOMENA.

"Miracles, in the sense of phenomena we cannot explain, surround us on every hand: life itself is the miracle of miracles."   George Bernard Shaw

———————————

OPENING UP TO SPIRIT-DIRECTED HEALING

If you want help from the realm of Unlimited Potential, you have to ask for it. The Beings of Light—called by many names—will then reach out and help you.

———————————

We[101] have described various phenomena and given explanations about how they might occur, and have given a personal interpretation of their significance to us and to people at large. Most phenomena, from orbs to crop circles, strangely moving lights or objects in the sky, unexplained light effects appearing on a photograph, unusual sound effects, are perhaps ways of the "Field of Unlimited Potential" trying to reach into our Earth sphere to get our attention. They likely want to assist us on our journey through life and toward greater consciousness, so it seems.

For ages, spiritual teachers have taught their students, "If you want help, you have to ask for it. Only then can the Beings of Light—called by many names—reach out and help you." Little children have no problem with doing just that. Their vivid imagination overcomes all borders and boundaries that cause us educated adults to doubt such wishful ways of thinking. Perhaps this explains the deeper meaning of the biblical statement of Master Jesus, "Unless you adopt the mind of children, you will not enter the Kingdom of God." This might suggest that lots of possibilities are closed to us when we only value those things that can be explained with the rational mind. To expand one's perception seems very important if one wishes to participate in life's full magnificence.

Looking back on our own journey, we can identify a continued expansion while we explored new places and met people from different cultures. Here is one such story. During our second year in California, and after many camping trips to national parks, we

———————————

[101] Gundi writes from her vantage point as healing arts practitioner.

followed an invitation to attend a week-long seminar in the near-by Santa Cruz mountains. The purpose of the seminar was to reflect upon our life, while taking time out from the business of everyday duties and responsibilities. It seemed, at the time, like a rather unusual vacation where most days were spent thinking about questions like "Where do I come from? Where am I going? What is the purpose of my life?"

However, to this day I cannot forget the change that took place as a result of this seminar. It was as if, after the week of reflection and intake of enriching spiritual material through talks and discussions, a new sense in our being had suddenly opened up. Returning home, the bushes and grasses in our backyard seemed greener. The flowers seemed brighter and more colorful than before. The sounds and forms around us seemed overwhelmingly beautiful, as if I saw them for the first time. The clouds in the sky, the songs of the birds, as well as the natural curiosity of our two preschool-age sons astounded and amazed us as never before. Everything seemed new, fresh, and more refined. Our outlook on life had changed. A transformation had occurred from within.

Several weeks after we attended this seminar, one of my brothers from Germany came to visit us for an extended stay. After some time, he commented, "What happened to you, sister? You look and act much younger and more joy-filled than I remember you!" His observation confirmed that transformation and expansion are possible if a person is exposed to inputs and experiences that promote this. The result is phenomenal.

BEING IN THE FLOW

"The truly rich person is one who is in contact with the energy of Love every second of his existence."　　　　　　　　　　　**Paulo Coelho**

———————————

During my training as healing arts practitioner, I met many empowered healers who encouraged us students to diligently follow the prescribed steps and trust that, in time, our hands would be able to sense more, and gain clear information from the person we scanned and wished to assist in healing. These teachers seemed to feel, sense, and intuit so much more than we beginners.

With great skepticism, yet optimistically trusting, I followed their advice. One teacher even said, "Don't expect big changes in the way of sensing energy for the next two years." That seemed to point to an apprenticeship of a very long time. However, I trusted, knowing that the healings do occur, and positive effects are granted from the Field of Unlimited Potential and can occur in spite of our personal limitations.

And so it was. The reports of my clients astounded me. They felt all kinds of positive changes and reactions, almost immediately. The field was working and producing miracles, as I willingly offered to be of service.

Then, one day, long before the second year had passed, my hands started buzzing the moment I moved them toward the client. The switch had been turned on. The energy was running full force. As if pulled by invisible strings, my hands were guided over the client's body. The timing of where to stay longer or shorter seemed directed from somewhere else. Even the words, if something needed to be said, seemed to flow in with certitude from this field of knowledge beyond. I knew intuitively when the work was completed and the session was to end.

When this new awareness became the norm, I was exhilarated and knew that I was working in concert with a greater power, which directed the process in all details, as I listened and allowed to follow the guidance as best as I knew how.

Like young children, freely expressing their wish list for Christmas, I dared to ask, "If you want me to do this work, send me clients and send those whom I can best serve with what I know now."

The request was answered. People made appointments, with issues for which I was ready and felt comfortable to deal with. Over time, this expanded in a natural way. I learned when to decline my services and delegate requests to specialists who seemed more qualified to help certain individuals.

To be in the flow of give and receive with the universal force feels like a creative dance, is a process of co-creating that uplifts and promotes "phenomenal" healing on many levels. It is a privilege and purpose at its best.

EXPERIENCING SPIRIT-DIRECTED HEALING

Over several decades we attended a variety of events with various masters of the healing arts. They all specialized in their unique approach or style. It seems fitting to describe the responses of people in these Spirit-directed healing events as "phenomenological."

Some people experience heat, or cold, or being struck by a shaft of light. Some are suddenly overcome by a waterfall of tears, or an outburst of uncontrollable laughter. Others feel that their body is like a reed being gently moved in the wind. People's knees might get soft, and they have to sit down or even lie down.

All this happens quite suddenly, as if touched by an invisible force. We ourselves experienced numerous times that willpower and a "firm stand" cannot withstand the touch of this Spirit energy. It's best to surrender, let go, and rest on the floor or seat. Eye lids might flutter, and cooling or warming energy might envelop the person for a short or extended period of time. Voices are heard in a distance, but they don't seem to matter as one rests in what feels like being in a cloud or cocoon of an unworldly experience. After some time, slowly natural sensations come back, and one knows the process is complete. One gets up and feels somehow renewed, relieved, knowing that one has been taken care of with what could be described as an energetic, uncontrollable experience of an unusual kind. The process varies from person to person. It is an unusual "phenomenon," and a wonderful energetic gift to be experienced at some point in a person's life.

"Look, if we can make crop circles, or UFOs, we can apply the same 'technology' to sustain you, and maintain your health and provide healing; this is what we are here to do."

It is noteworthy and, perhaps, most significant to examine if the very same explanation—i.e., that the subtle energy available to conscious nonphysical beings to imprint orbs in photo cameras or make crop circles or even UFOs—can also be applied to healing of biological cells, i.e., to the phenomenon of spirit directed healing.

In our previous books we have described that intelligent application of subtle energies, such as those used to imprint orbs in digital photos, can have enough physical power to change or correct the programming of biological cells. We argued that this might be possible when they are concentrated directly onto the specific locations within the individual biological cells that are determinative for their overall functionality.

We explained this with four characteristics of orbs which we had derived from our studies of the orb phenomenon:

(a) They are made with very little energy—as few as only several hundred photons impinging on the photographic charge plate of the camera.

(b) They can move exceedingly fast—we argued that even the speed of light might not be a limitation for them.

(c) They can change their size very fast, from quite large to super-tiny—meaning that their energy "density," i.e., the number of photons hitting per unit area, can be quite high when focused onto a tiny area,[102] certainly high enough to affect the status of chemical bonds.

(d) They can be directed at will by the nonphysical intelligence behind the orb phenomenon.

In terms of the energetics involved, this would be a plausible mechanism for making crop circles. There we hypothesized that the cells at or immediately above the nodal points on the grain stems are reprogrammed such that the stem bends at that point, typically several centimeters above grade. It will likely take reprogramming a multitude of cells to obtain the bending of one single grain stem, as well as intelligence to do this at the right point in the correct direction, but both the energy and the intelligence are plentifully available in the nonphysical reality, and the speed to accomplish all this, stem by stem, in infinitesimal time is no problem, either.

Additionally, the fact that tens of thousands of those single grain stems are involved in the making of a crop circle, and they often exhibit a stunning, intricate pattern over an area of the size of a football field, indicates that there is enormous intelligence behind all this. It shows that that which designs and "manifests" the crop circle—that which might emanate the orbs to do this—is truly powerful.

Similarly, we can consider that there is an exceedingly high degree of intelligence that can manifest and direct orbs in an effective process of phenomenal physical healing. In very rapid succession, but in a distinct cell by cell sequential approach, all those billions of

---

[102] This can simplistically be likened a magnifying glass which, if you hold it in just the right position with respect to the sun and a piece of paper, can focus the entirety of the sun rays falling on the lens onto a tiny spot in the focal plane of the lens, which would then receive so much locally concentrated energy that it will burn a hole in the paper. As another example, I have, in my professional work in surface physics, performed *in-situ* transmission electron microscopy studies of gas reactions on surfaces, where I concentrated the imaging electron beam—very similar to light rays but more energetic—onto selected small areas of the "specimen" which I was studying, and by doing so heated the specific irradiated areas—which were much smaller than a biological cell—by several hundred degrees.

affected cells that have lost their proper programming and contributed to a disease can be "visited" and "treated" by the orb(s), and healed. The healing could be by pointing their subtle energy power to exactly the right spot in the cell, such as to supply just the right amount of energy to re-establish a broken chemical bond, or to correct some other programming problem, or by "burning up" the cell entirely, so it will no longer negatively affect its environment. This sort of "cell by cell corrective action" can be hypothesized as the underlying "mechanism" by which spirit-directed healing occurs. It would be very similar to how crop circles are made, and, in principle, not much different from how apparitions, or even UFOs, are manifested in a person's mind.

Key to all of this is the understanding that in the nonphysical reality, where phenomena such as spirit-directed healing originate, all wisdom and all medical and technical knowledge that has ever been developed is stored and is instantaneously accessible to those entities who perform the healing. This accessibility is available to entities who lived on Earth (or another planet) and deceased recently, or hundreds or thousands of years ago, or even to those entities who never incorporated into a physical life. They would be equally "intelligent" and "qualified" to perform any healing of any physical challenge; they tap into the same knowledge base at the "Hall of Records."[103] In the nonphysical reality, from where they operate, no medical education would be needed—all knowledge is instantaneously at their avail.

We have pragmatically discussed this phenomenological spiritual healing process in detail in the Afterword of *The Orb Project* (in a chapter titled *The Hypothesis for Divine Healing*), as well as in Chapter 12—*Spiritual Healing*—of *Orbs, their Mission and Messages of Hope*. Additionally, in their book *Beyond UFOs, the Science of*

---

[103] The term "Hall of Records" was borrowed from Sylvia Brown (e.g., in her book *Phenomenon – Everything you need to know about the Paranormal*).

Consciousness and Contact with Non-Human Intelligence,[104] Rey Hernandez et al. present a similar phenomenological explanation of spiritual healing. They studied a large number of individual non-human intelligence "experiencer" reports and suggest that "nonhuman intelligent beings appear to operate individually and seemingly *en-masse* in a state of consciousness very different from that possessed by those of us on earth at the present time."

Hernandez *et a.* do make the inference that "orbs" may be involved in the human experience of such healings, but they do not make a clear distinction between nonhuman "extraterrestrial" and "nonphysical/ spiritual" intelligence and/or beings. In my understanding, as described in the previous chapter on UFOs and ETs, there is an all-important difference between those. Extraterrestrial intelligence is based on physical existence of some sort; nonphysical/spiritual intelligence is free of mass or matter.

At this point I want to remind the reader of the question we asked at the end of Chapter 4.2 on *Crop Circles*, "Might there be an intentional connection between crop circles and spirit-directed healing? Might one of the reasons for the emergence of crop circles be to communicate that physical healing is what the unseen reality is not only capable of, but also actively doing?"

Think about it: Is there anything for us humans that is more important than health? There is not, and nothing more needs to be said to emphasize this point. Given this undeniable realization, humanity has—likely in more books than have ever been published on any other topic, in more conferences than on any other subject, with higher expense than for any other concern—addressed the questions over and over again, "What is it that governs our health? What is it that sustains our health?"

No matter how enormous our human achievements have been in the health sector, we have not even begun to understand what

---

[104] Rey Hernandez, Jon Klimo, and Rudy Schild, May 2018, FREE - private communication

it is that gives us life and sustains it. Life energy is as mysterious as it has ever been. Our universities are cranking out 20,000 MDs every year,[105] each one of them calling a "doctoral thesis" their own that adds to the overall knowledge in medicine. And comparatively an equal number of PHD theses in physics, chemistry, biology and similar subject areas are written each year that are funded with NIH (National Institute of Health) grants and similar public funds. And we still are at a loss when it comes to fundamental insights why some people succumb to a stroke, contract terminal cancer, commit suicide, or become Alzheimer's victims far too early in their lives, while they follow their doctors' guidelines for living healthy, yet others live "normal" lives, eat and drink what's available and what they like, and happily live into their 90s or 100s in good health.

We simply don't know the secrets that govern these basic circumstances of life. We are unaware of the bigger picture within which each of us lives his/her life. We construct theories why this and that is good for us, but we do not take into consideration the over-reaching priorities of the reality which sustains our lives. We don't understand that, when a child is dying of cancer, a young mother is being killed in a car accident, a joyful doctor of chiropractic succumbs to a cancer that "normally" carries a high survival probability, or when 3000 people are getting killed in an insane act of terror or in a natural disaster, that this may well be an acceptable occurrence in the "Scheme of Everything." We simply don't understand that, when it comes to "life" and "health," the *Unseen Reality* is determinative.

This is, we submit, where phenomena come into play. Once we have made the one and only necessary leap of faith—which is actually supported by a huge amount of evidence—that there is conscious, loving life on the other side of the vail, we can then look at phenomena as attempts by conscious entities in that realm to make us aware of their existence and of their intent to help and guide us through this ever so short period of time which we call life.

---

[105] See Tab. B-2.2 in "Total Graduates by U.S. Medical School and Sex, 2013-2014 through 2017-2018." Aamc.org.

In our discussion of *Spirit Orbs* we have concluded that they carry loving messages to the effect that there are unseen helpers around us who care for our health. We even have some phenomenological ideas how they can do this. We have also hypothesized that the same purpose and intention, a "We can do it!" notion, may be behind the crop circle phenomenon, and perhaps even behind UFO-experiences. It is as if "They" want to say to us, "Look, if we can make these crop circles, we can apply the same 'technology' to sustain you, and maintain your health and provide healing; this is what we are here to do."

As we stated earlier, a plausible scientific explanation for genuine crop circles would be that some sort of other-worldly consciousness-driven application of subtle energies is used for re-programming biological cells to affect the bending of the tens of thousands of grain stems in the crop circle. The same can be done with cells in the human body. There is no fundamental difference.

This may well mean that the primary purpose of crop circles is to demonstrate to us that intention-directed other-worldly focus can be used for physical healing of people who are afflicted with health challenges. One would be just as easy for "Them" as the other. This is spirit-directed healing.

5.   WHAT DOES ALL THIS TELL US?

It is possible to energetically imprint distinct patterns in the mind of people, just as easily as it is to imprint orbs on a photographic charge plate, or affect kinking in grains in the making of crop circles, or make cell programming corrections in human organs in the process which we call "spirit-directed healing.

In this chapter of the book we elaborate that phenomena can lead us to a new world view—a new concept of the spiritual realm. After a detailed description of what this world view might entail, we talk about the ramifications for us humans and for our planet at large.

As human beings, we are instruments for the evolution of cosmic consciousness, and as such we take part in evolving the very essence of the underlying **Grand Original Design**.

Given this realization, our planet—even though it is likely only one among many similar ones in the Universe that evolves/evolved highly intelligent living species—is an utmost precious cosmic commodity. Preserving it as basis for the continued evolution of consciousness for many future generations is, therefore, of high importance. We argue that this may well be a key message which is intended to be imparted to us by those in the nonphysical realm who originate the spectrum of phenomena we discuss in this book.

A NEW WORLD VIEW

———————————

My most important learning from our experience with the orb phenomenon has been that it shattered my antiquated world view and taught me that a reality beyond the physical realm really does exist and is very different from what I had heretofore assumed, which was based on—or strongly influenced by—my Christian-based belief system.

I had never abandoned my conviction that something deeply profound and sacred exists in connection with this "life experience." But it had become clear to me already as early as in my upper high school years that the worldview of my upbringing is fundamentally flawed. GOD, I reckoned, must be more than some sort of invisible super-human figure somewhere in the endless skies above or beneath us. It cannot be that GOD loves some people and condemns others. Divine love must be expected to be indiscriminately extended to everybody! This is an irrefutable spiritual law! There is no such thing as heaven, or eternal condemnation, where some people's souls find themselves after death. These are human constructs. I had given up this unsatisfactory world view decades ago. But what exactly replaced it had mostly remained undefined.

The orb phenomenon gave me a new, direct understanding of the possibilities and capabilities of the spiritual realm. When I realized that the orb phenomenon cannot be fully explained with the "wisdom" of conventional natural sciences, I knew that this is, at least to me, undeniable evidence for the existence of a reality beyond.

Specific conclusions from our orbs research then gave me insights into some of the characteristics of that reality:

- **Energetics:** many orders of magnitude lower energies than typical physical energies; the energies to imprint an orb are of the order of 10^{-16} Ampere-seconds, which is in the "subtle energy" range; yet with proper application, such minute physical energies can be exceedingly effective.
- **Velocities:** not limited by the speed of light; velocities in the spiritual realm may be many orders of magnitude faster than the speed of light.
- **Time and Space:** there is temporal and spatial omnipresence, as seen from the human perspective; yet processes defining "before" and "after" situations still exist.
- **Information Decay:** information exists in perpetuity; there is no decay.
- **Intelligence:** vastly superior access to the knowledge accumulated over the ages; due to super-high processing speeds and absence of information decay, any information about anything that has ever been experienced, sensed, calculated, invented, achieved is stored and essentially instantaneously retrievable.
- **Individualism:** there is individuality also in the reality beyond.
- **Wisdom:** much greater than in the physical reality, but nonetheless evolving.
- **Intent:** indiscriminately offering help; making every possible attempt to do so.
- **Method:** intelligently and incessantly trying to get our attention for their messages.
- **Communication:** direct, scientific verifiable inter-reality communication is not permitted.

This gave me the freedom to cast away the antiquated, unrealistic, unfitting Judeo-Christian *"Gestalt"* of my childhood belief system. It replaced it with a much more majestic, all-encompassing world view than I had ever heretofore believed was possible and permissible. It culminates with the new understanding that we are part of a consciousness-evolving universe, part of a "**Grand Original Design**" that evolves itself with the help of its own creation, designed such that each element in it contributes to the further enhancement of the whole. Simplistically yet poignantly phrased, this means that "you and I are evolving GOD. We are co-creators."

When we humans think in terms of "big" and "small" we are fundamentally limiting our understanding of Reality.

Confirmation that man is participating in the Evolution of GOD is a conclusion I drew just from our research into the Orb Phenomenon. What if we expand our conclusion beyond just the orb phenomenon? What if we include the phenomenon of crop circles? Or spiritual healing? What about UFOs? Are there similarities? Are these also of the same, spirit-intended, or spirit-directed origin? Is their intent the same, i.e., indiscriminately wanting to help us, and humankind at large? Are these other phenomena also primarily intended to convey messages from the unseen world?

Orbs are small features in digital photographs. To "manufacture" an orb takes as little as about 10^{-16} Ampere-seconds of physical energy, which is very, very little energy, essentially "nothing" when looked at from the frame of mind of the physical reality.[106] On the other hand, crop circles are comparatively huge physical structures, sometimes more than 500 feet in size. Yet they are incredibly intricate! To produce them appears to require many orders of magnitude more physical energy than what it takes to produce an orb. But is this really so?

It may certainly appear that way. Indeed, if we liken the mechanism to make a crop circle to people walking in the field and stampeding patterns onto the grains, bending them down perhaps with some snow-shoe like boards tied to their feet, that would indeed take a comparatively enormous amount of physical energy. But to make genuine crop circles, rather than such "fake" ones, could be

---

[106] I first published about this in an article entitled *The Orb Phenomenon: bridging to the world beyond?* in the British journal *Light* (College of Psychic Studies, Spring 2013; see *http://www.theheinemanns.net/Light5-13.pdf*).

accomplished with far less energy. I suspect that genuine crop circles are produced by intelligent re-programming of cells located at the point where the grains are being bent. This would be non-human action. The type of energy required to do that would be what we call "subtle" energy, which is of the order of one billionth of one billionth of the magnitude of comparative physical energy and is very much in the realm of possibilities of what entities in the non-physical realm can do.

Could it be that there is a teaching? Could it be that we are to learn from studying orbs and crop circles that physical size does not matter when it comes to the spirit realm? Could the teaching be to make us understand that, when we humans think in terms of "big" and "small," we are fundamentally limiting our understanding of Reality? Are we receiving a lesson in thinking new, without preconception— without thinking that "big" is big and "small" is small? Are we being given a demonstration how limited our human thinking really is?

Indeed, we perceive orbs and crop circles as very different because of their size differences. New thinking indicates that, in the reality where the non-human intelligence resides that manifests these physical phenomena, size as we know it does not matter. Consciousness has nothing to do with physical size. Its manifestation has nothing to do with that. The microcosm and macrocosm are equally fascinating.[107] Yet our thinking has not adapted to this truth.[108]

---

[107] My academic training was in both these fields of science, astronomy and atomic-resolution electron microscopy. Striking similarities in the structure of the macroscopic and microscopic worlds always fascinated me.

[108] Throughout our book *Expanding Perception* we discuss this topic at some length, trying to dismiss the false, antiquated understanding that "larger is better."

ADAPTING TO THE HUMAN PERSPECTIVE

We are all subject to personal conditioning. In their great wisdom, the non-human intelligence that is all around us, but invisible to us, tries to get our attention with whatever means we can perceive them most readily.

Another finding of our research into Phenomena has been to simply realize that the entities of non-human intelligence are able to adapt to whichever form will grab our diversified human attention. Some people are impressed with the large size of crop circles. Others with their intricacies. Yet others are fascinated seeing small orbs in their photographs. Among those, some will be especially intrigued if they see faces inside the orbs; others if they see beautiful mandala-like interiorities; and yet others if they see the orbs in other than circular shapes. Some see little gnomes, others animal-like features that they interpret as their power guide. Still others see apparitions of Saints that are particularly meaningful to them, or they see UFOs or even ETs. It is all a matter of perspective, acquired by personal conditioning. In their great wisdom, the non-human intelligent beings that are all around us but invisible to us try to get our attention with whatever means we can perceive them most readily. They will make great efforts—within the realm of their possibilities—to meet the perceived expectation.

And then there are numerous other phenomenological experiences that we have not even discussed in the preceding subchapters, through which beings of non-human intelligence might want to get our attention, such as near-death experiences ("NDEs"), abductions, astral travel, past life flash-backs, certain other dream states, ET encounters, etc. etc. The human condition is exceedingly diverse. Not one person is the same as another. Our tastes, preferences, views, understandings are all different, we all have preconceptions that stem from our personal conditioning.

None of this is particularly good or bad, they are just different. For one, a glass is half full, for another the same glass is half empty. For one the contents of the glass is delicious, another finds it distasteful. Hence, the ideal approach to get our attention is different for each person. And what we are seeing when studying phenomena is that the entities creating them know how to tailor them individually, so we will best notice them.

What I have personally learned from looking at seemingly vastly different phenomena is that, since the orb phenomenon is for real, and the crop circle phenomenon is also genuine, probably numerous other phenomena should then also be authentic. I particularly emphasize here the phenomenon of spirit-directed healing! Once we have given credence to orbs, crop circles, apparitions, or UFOs or ETs, or NDEs or alike, we can no longer simply look at other ones, such as spirit-directed healing, with comparatively more skepticism. That would be illogical.

THE IMMENSITY OF THE GRAND ORIGINAL DESIGN

The UFO phenomenon offers a new perspective of the grandeur of the Divine Plan, which provided for the seeds for countless independent consciousness-generating civilizations in the Universe.

The question remains, why is there, apparently, all this attention directed from the nonphysical world toward us? Looking at the UFO and ET phenomenon, we have learned that individual humans like ourselves are small microcosms in a vast universe. Why then would it be important for non-human Entities to help us and make us aware that they are caring for us? If we are insignificant, why would they bother?

The fact that they do show interest in us indicates that, even though small, we do have a not-insignificant role in the "scheme of everything." It is an evolutionary role, and it is tied to consciousness. As insignificant as we are, we are instruments for the evolution of cosmic consciousness, and as such we take part in evolving the very essence of the underlying **Grand Original Design**. We have touched on this earlier in this book, and we have said much about it in "Expanding Perception"—we recommend to revert to that book to read more about this train of thought.

In particular looking into the UFO phenomenon has given me a new perspective of the grandeur of the Divine Plan, which included the seeds for countless independent consciousness-generating civilizations in the Universe. Each is a fantastic "creation project" in its own right.[109] There is no way for any one of them to interact

---

[109] It is, for example, not necessary for living organisms to be built on carbon as basic element. It is conceivable that, given the appropriate temperature and atmospheric conditions, organisms with quite different chemistries could evolve— for instance, involving other classes of carbon compounds, or compounds of another element, such as silicon, or another solvent in place of water. Already back in my undergraduate years, I recall an exciting organic chemistry class where these

with any other. Each has been given the possibility to evolve, unfold in its own way. Each one learns to deal with adversities as they come up. Each expands uniquely in consciousness and contributes uniquely to cosmic consciousness. And also, given the likelihood of fundamentally different biochemistry principles prevailing on different planets in the universe, actual interaction—such as meeting up, if it were possible—would be biologically and technically exceedingly problematic.

I am reminded of what Gundi and I experienced on a travel to the Galapagos Islands. The creatures living on these islands evolved without influence from other parts of the world. The human footprint was not part of their evolution. There were no human predators to run away from. The element of being afraid of humans, who would chase them away from their habitat, or kill them for food, or domesticate them, has been absent. The result has been that birds and iguanas and seals and multitudes of living species live in harmony side by side. I remember the eerie feeling when we stepped among them, very carefully trying not to inconvenience any one of them – but they were not afraid. The birds would not fly away, we were immediately accepted in their midst as non-threatening other "creatures."

Don't you sometimes wonder how elevated civilizations on other planets in the Universe might evolve? How would they deal with territoriality? With greed? Do they develop weapons to keep each other in check? Are weapons of mass destruction inventions of humanity alone? What about money? Did they invent the use of money on other civilized planets? How do their "people" look and feel like? How does their environment look like? Do they have a variety of plants and animals similar to ours? Do they have colorful flowers, seasons, and cloud formations and sun and moonshine? Do they have books and libraries, and computers and Radio and TV? How are they governed? Do they have countries and borders and

---

possibilities of alternate biochemistry were discussed. See also *"Hypothetical Types of Biochemistry"* in Wikipedia.

military forces? Do they have racism, ideologies, religions? Do they have refugees? What are their joys of life? How long is their life span?

You can continue this sort of questioning *ad libitum*. And when you find yourself pondering them, are you not filled with *AWE* about our own planet, about the beauty, and the endless variety of amenities life offers us? Let your mind wander around that which you have already seen and experienced in your life. Is that not grandiose? You might wish take time out and look at "Magnificence" in http://www.healingguidance.net/magnificence/, or find the wealth of similar information about the beauty of our nature on the Internet, offered by many others.

CONCERN ABOUT THE HEALTH OF OUR PLANET

"As we grow in our consciousness, there will be more compassion and more love, and then the barriers between people, between religions, between nations will begin to fall."
Ram Dass

We have earlier pointed out that a primary purpose of the crop circle phenomenon and, perhaps of orbs may well be to demonstrate that intention-directed other-worldly focus can be used for physical healing of people who are afflicted with health challenges. Imprinting orbs on photo media, or crop circles on large corn fields, would be just as easy for "entities in the spiritual realm" as reprogramming of cells in human beings for curing health challenges.

The messages which Entities in the nonphysical reality are trying to convey may, in fact, go far beyond all that. They may want to wake us up, shake us, tell us that they can do "anything." They can see where we are going as a species on this planet, and they may want to entice us to stop the foolishness with which we treat the gem which is our own planet. They may want to tell us to put an end to the injustice with which we treat each other. They may want us to think about values, make us aware, understand that there is more to *Life* than we ever thought life would be. They may wish to teach us gratitude, appreciation, thankfulness, [agape-type] love. They may want us to become aware of the numerous detrimental causes which numb our minds, so we might experience truth, beauty, and goodness once again …

When we consider that the reality in which these Entities reside has no spatial and temporal constraints, we can conclude that *they* have instantaneous access to all experiences and all consciousness that has ever been "produced" on Earth, or even in the Universe. It is like having a "cosmic Internet" at their avail, infinitely more powerful than our worldly Internet, in that it is not bandwidth-limited and has all information that has ever been experienced available for instantaneous retrieval—perhaps not to all entities in that reality, but certainly to the higher evolved ones.[110]

With that capability, it is fathomable that they can come to conclusions which we, in our physical space-time constraint, would call "predicting future occurrences."[111] They may be seeing that we are on a path of great harm to ourselves, or of destruction of our Earth which is the very basis for continued evolution of consciousness on this planet, and they may be wanting to warn us and implore us to correct our course so this otherwise inevitable outcome is avoided. Are they making us aware of impending changes in our living conditions for which we have to be prepared? What we know today about the global challenges facing our planet, such as the dangers of global warming, nuclear energy production, overpopulation, natural catastrophes, and alike suggests such an interpretation.

We cannot help but point out the obvious, which is that much more is at stake. With the potential of massive conventional and cruel nuclear and biological warfare with which we humans have decided to defend our territorial claims on the beauty of this planet, we now have the power to annihilate not only most every "thing" which

---

[110] While it is not critical for the point we are making, we note that some people liken the "unseen reality" to our own with regard to the multitude of varieties it offers, all the way from very low to very highly evolved individual spirits. They also attribute a hierarchical structure to that reality, perhaps much more so than we find in the physical reality. Certainly, the noble causes we describe here refer to the highly evolved spirits.

[111] A "prediction into the future" can be understood as a series of logical extrapolations of a multitude of situations that have actually happened. We apply this, for example, routinely in the medical field. We look at a particular health challenge, try to correlate it with as many other personal data we can get a hold of, then convolute it with similar cases that have been experienced by other patients in similar situations, and come up with a prognosis, i.e., a prediction of the likely course of events with regard to this health challenge, and of the likelihood that a certain treatment protocol will cure or remit the problem. It is reasonable to assume that all this sort of information will instantaneously be available to "specialists" in the nonphysical reality, and that this becomes the basis for prediction of future events.

humanity has created over the centuries, but also every living being along with it. The Entities on the other side of the veil may want to wake us up and confront us with the fact that we have entirely lost sight of any reasoning. They look at what has led to all this and see that the most cruel wars which humanity has been fighting originate from a wrong interpretation of our spiritual origins, of what we call "religion." From their perspective, it must be saddening to see that the love they are extending to us is, due to our ignorance, paradoxically becoming the very reason why we kill rather than love and respect each other.

Will we recognize the karmic knot which mankind finds itself in, and accept the gifts from the other side to solve it? It seems to me that nothing less is at stake, and that we are being shown that healing on this huge scale is possible.

WHY COMMUNICTION VIA PHENOMENA?

It is part of the Grand Original Design that phenomena are the most direct means of communication between the spiritual and physical realities.

We have talked extensively about the desire of highly evolved entities in the nonphysical reality to communicate certain messages to us. Why would they want to do this? Why would they not just leave us alone, with all the problems we are having? We are probably in their eyes not much more than an ant colony would be for us—and, by comparison, we would typically not be super-interested in helping an ant to particularly thrive, would we?

We have discussed that one of perhaps many methods for "Them" to communicate with us is via phenomena. The question then arises, why do they use such a complicated method? If they really want to help us, why don't they just tell us outright what to do? Why do they not communicate more directly with us, or to us? Why do they not "command" us to do this or that, or behave this and not that way?

This set of questions is not trivial. There is more to it than just the obvious lack of physical audibility with regard to that which they might wish to tell us. After all, since these nonhuman entities are nonphysical, they have no physical/biological means to produce sound that we can perceive with our ears—via air pressure waves— or direct mail or emails from God that we can read.

The deeper reason for this inability of direct communication is that, for good reason, it is part of the **Grand Original Design** not to permit more direct communication. We have dealt with this in *Expanding Perception* but consider it so important for the context of this book that we will summarize the rationale here again.

As we see it, the purpose of life on our planet, as well as of civilizations on other planets in the Universe, is to generate consciousness and, hence, participate in the evolution of that which created all that is. Consciousness is not knowledge. It is more than that. It is a noble quality that can more appropriately be described as "knowledge in context."[112] We can study for years and years, we can learn much of what there is to learn, but that does not make us conscious. It may help, but consciousness is not a necessary end product of knowledge. Consciousness has to do with what we do with the knowledge we have acquired. It is more closely related to wisdom; it includes the non-rational faculties of the mind, such as feeling, compassion, love.[113]

---

[112] This is actually the etymology of the word "consciousness": It is derived from the Latin "*conscire*" which means "*to know together with,*" to "*know in context* [of something larger];" "*to know* [as deep truth] *within oneself.*"

[113] See Appendix (B) for more about what we define as "consciousness" in this context.

BEING CO-CREATORS

> **It is not enough to obey, we must initiate. Whatever we do, if it is to count as a contribution to cosmic consciousness, we must do it out of free will.**

The highly evolved entities on the other side of the veil understand, as we pointed out, that the purpose of humanity—and of all other conscious civilizations on multitudes of other planets in the galaxies of the Universe—is to enhance the very essence of that which created everything. We are to co-create by contributing to the field of consciousness. This cannot be done by *them* simply telling us what to do. We must decide, on the basis on free choices between alternatives! A step of decision-making must be built in. It is up to us to become conscious in any situation. If they were to tell us, in no uncertain terms, what we must do, we would be foolish not to follow through with doing that. We may then well be doing something "good" as a result of obeying, but that action does not advance consciousness.[114]

In this time of the history of mankind, it is not enough to obey, we must initiate.

How then does this relate to phenomenal prophecies? The other day I was introduced to a person who has a very unusual gift. In what he describes as a "dream state" he receives information about future events. He has predicted airplane crashes, political assassinations, terrorist attacks, outcomes of elections, natural disasters, and alike with extreme precision, such as names and dates and times, the number of fatalities, and other special circumstances, all from several months to years into the future. The track record of his predictions is astonishing. When given the opportunity to consult a person who has the gift of making such precise predictions, how should I respond?

----

[114] In Appendix (B) we explain in more depth what we mean when we talk about "consciousness."

Over time, the world has known a number of human beings who had the indisputable gift of predicting future events. Several years ago, Gundi and I visited the Nostradamus museum in Salon-de-Provence in Southern France, where the famous astrologer, physician, and seer *Michel de Nostredame* (1503-1566) worked almost five centuries ago. He is famous for having made stunning predictions that would extend more than 400 years into the future, all the way into our modern times.[115]

For me, these examples of an ability to predict future events are affirmative evidence of the existence of a spiritual reality, as we discussed in this book. But they are not normal. They seem to fit in the **G**rand **O**riginal **D**esign only as exceptions, not the rule.[116] The "rule" states that we are not supposed to be given insight into clear-cut predictions of future events. We will advance consciousness by reflective, objective, altruistic evaluation of the alternatives presented to us in any given important situation, unencumbered by credible predictions about their outcome which would tell us how beneficial the decision will turn out for us.

Nonetheless, certain prophecies do have their place. The last two words of the preceding paragraph, "for us," are key. If we were able to unquestionably only have the greater good in mind, without any entanglement with personal interests, it can well be argued that predictions of future events should be pursued.

Diligence and Discernment are absolutely needed when it comes to the evaluation of prophecies that might serendipitously come to our attention. Once they have passed the test of discernment, certain prophecies are then acceptable means of communication between the nonphysical reality and mankind. We should add that they are quite seldom, indeed. It seems that the divine reality will use them only in occasions, when they see an occurrence developing that is

---

[115] In the mid 1550s Nostradamus published predictions about our current era, many of which have been proven astonishingly correct.

[116] A proverb pointedly states, "The exception proves the rule."

of particular importance to them with regard to the continuity of the **Grand Original Design**.

In most other situations, which arise much more frequently, when individuals who portend to be able to see into the future offer "readings" to other people, often for a significant fee, utmost discernment is advised. On our path toward higher consciousness—toward being effective co-creators—we need to diligently base our actions on decisions for the "nobler" of true alternatives presented to us, not on authoritative predictions. The **Grand Original Design** generally provides that a separation—a red line that cannot be crossed—must be maintained between us humans and what entities in the nonphysical reality can unequivocally tell us to do.[117] Whatever we do, if it is to count as a contribution to consciousness, we must do it out of free will. Being co-creators means that we must be the initiators. We must ourselves decide to do it, out of a state of respect, compassion, love of something or someone outside ourselves. Knowledge alone cannot be the basis for consciousness. Accordingly, it would be within the purview of the **Grand Original Design** that they give us hunches, or clues, but they are not "permitted" to give us crystal-clear orders. That would be a violation of the set-up of the **Grand Original Design**. A finite degree of uncertainty, of mystery, must remain.

The "Design" is such that those who do not believe in intellectually unexplainable occurrences can justify and choose to remain unconvinced, without detriment to their well-being, while the rest of us are welcome to find exciting meaning in the phenomena being presented to us.

---

[117] See also the chapter entitled *The Orb/EVP Experiment* in Appendix (C).

6. APPENDIX

APPENDIX (A)
The Energy → Consciousness Process

Consciousness is the end-product of a two-step "divine creative process" that involves the physical and spiritual realities. With this ingenious concept, the **Grand Original Design** elevated humans to become co-creators: GOD is evolving Itself with the help of its own creation.

APPENDIX (B)
Consciousness

A computer will never be a producer of consciousness in and by itself. Consciousness has nothing to do with mental output, or a high IQ, or academic degrees, but it has everything to do with living an honest, joyful, compassionate, meaningful and fulfilling life.

APPENDIX (C)
The Orb/EVP Experiment

No matter how much we would strive for certainty about the life hereafter, we will not get certainty about it. Mystery must remain. We are given signs and hints and lots of active help from the other side, but the "when" and "how" and "to whom" and "how much" will remain "Their" prerogative, not ours. Signs are being communicated as phenomena, not facts.

APPENDIX (D)
Recommendations for Orb Photography

Orbs are not objects to "hunt" for, but phenomena given to us, to ask for. Use a conventional, inexpensive point-and-shoot digital camera with flash and CCD-sensor; use the built-in or an external flash; choose clean environmental conditions; shoot series of photos against a darkened uniform background, and ask for the privilege of seeing orb messengers.

APPENDIX (A)

THE ENERGY → CONSCIOUSNESS PROCESS

The only "realistic" way to communicate from the spiritual to the physical reality is via what we call phenomena, i.e., via effects that are not scientifically reproducible and not verifiable. This is one of the most ingenious aspects of the Grand Original Design.

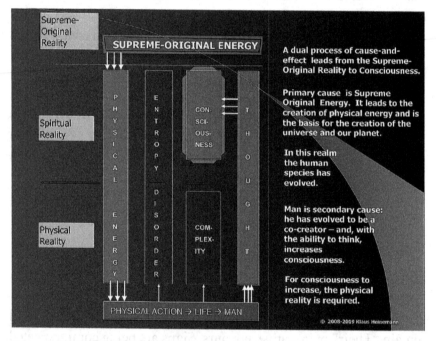

Photo 12: Flow chart of the cosmic/divine energy-consciousness process. By **G**rand **O**riginal **D**esign, Supreme Original energy is converted for the creation of the physical reality (the universe), which becomes the basis for species capable of reflective thought and eventually consciousness to evolve.

The concept of the manuscript I found myself writing back in 1979 during our family winter vacation culminated with the description of an Energy → Consciousness process pointing out that the human being is designed to be nothing less than a vehicle to further evolve that which God is.[118] The train of thought can be summarized in essentially four parts:

(1) We start with an extrapolation of a basic law in quantum physics. We hypothesize that Reality at large is composed of two parts that relate to each other similar to the particle-wave dualism. The entire physical reality—everything, from the subatomic particle to the farthest corner of the most distant galaxy in the universe—would be comparable to the particle dualism aspect; and an unseen reality, which we initially simply called "counterpart reality" and later equated with what people typically call the "spiritual reality," would be comparable to the wave dualism aspect. Drawing from the differences between particles and waves in physics, we conclude that the major characteristics of the counterpart/ spiritual reality would be velocities up to many magnitudes greater than the speed of light, which essentially means that we approach independence of time and space within that reality, when compared to the physical reality. It also means that the spiritual reality does not contain physical mass. The physical and the spiritual realities are duals of what we call the *Supreme Original Reality*, and they function according to the *Grand Original Design*.

(2) Consciousness[119] is the end-product of a two-step "creative process" that involves the physical and spiritual realities to work. The first step started in the supreme original reality and is what we commonly describe as the "Big Bang," i.e., the singular event that most scientists agree occurred some 13.7 billion years ago, when a quantum of supreme-original energy was converted into physical energy and, hence, into physical mass or matter, which is a state of physical energy.

---

[118] This entire concept is described in much more detail in the Appendix to Expanding Perception.

[119] See Appendix (B) for our understanding of this important word "Consciousness," as used in the context of this book.

This conversion process included the potential for biological matter and ultimately human life on Earth—and similar life on many other earth-like planets elsewhere in our galaxy and beyond—to evolve. The second creative step comprises that the highest evolved biological species—the human being on planet Earth—has attained the power of reflective thought and has the potential to apply thought and experience to "create" consciousness, which is the intended outcome.

(3) This entire process has been consuming a huge amount of physical energy, until it was finally possible to produce this intended outcome. In physics, consumed energy is called entropy. Hence, we have a "process of increasing entropy and increasing consciousness" as duals of something we can call the *Supreme Creation Process*. Consciousness, the intended outcome of the supreme creation process, can only be achieved in this dual-step process that involves intelligent physical/biological beings in the physical universe. We define the combined total of all consciousness created by sentient beings as "Cosmic Consciousness." The **Grand Original Design**, with which the Big Bang was empowered, included all this potentiality for the creation of individual and cosmic consciousness.

The **Grand Original Design** included its own evolution to ever-increasing cosmic consciousness: GOD is evolving itself, and man is a vehicle for this to happen.

(4) The speed of light is the dividing line between the physical and spiritual realities. The **Grand Original Design** ingeniously provides that this barrier cannot easily be crossed in either direction. Breaking this barrier from the physical to the spiritual reality realm is practically prohibited for anything that contains physical mass/matter. We have used this basic law of physics when we discussed that the probability for any two intelligent civilizations in the universe to ever be

able to meet and communicate with each other is essentially zero. Any argumentation that biological beings, which by definition encompass physical mass or matter, could ever travel faster than at the speed of light must be considered impossible. Crossing the barrier from the spiritual to the physical reality is possible but, since the former does not contain any mass or matter, the effect of crossing this veil is not easily materially manifested in the physical reality, and therefore not easily detectable by beings in the physical reality, i.e., our five senses do not include the unambiguous capability of such detection. Manifestations do occur under certain circumstances, but their appearance is subject to uncertainty and unpredictability, similar to the uncertainty principle in quantum physics; and their interpretation is not determinative but subject to personal/scientific interpretation.

The only "realistic" way to communicate from the spiritual to the physical reality is, therefore, via what we call phenomena, i.e., via effects that are not reproducible and not verifiable. This is arguably the most ingenious aspect of the **G**rand **O**riginal **D**esign. If, in fact, communication from the spiritual dimension to us were clear and precise, if there were no place for doubt or mysticism, then "hunches" would be facts, and following them would have nothing to do with consciousness but would simply be a matter of course, or logic. Consciousness involves a personal decision for something good outside of ourselves—a decision for a nobler alternative, as our teacher Harry Rathbun called it. For this to happen, we must place love over knowledge, compassion over righteousness.

APPENDIX (B)

CONSCIOUSNESS

Consciousness cannot be produced by a computer; it has nothing to do with mental output, or academic degrees, but it has everything to do with living a joyful, meaningful, fulfilling life.

The other day I (KH) was reading a scholarly 2004 paper by our late friend Virginia Essene about the latest insights into the development of the human brain. After a while, my mind started to spin around the analogy between the human brain and a computer. Likening a human brain to a computer is certainly nothing new. But some aspects do intrigue me.

A computer can be divided into three aspects: hardware, software, and applications. The first two are quite straight-forward, and nothing much needs to be said about them. "Hardware" comprises the entire device, including the processors, the memory chips, the storage devices—everything that you take home from the Apple Store when you purchase your new computer. "Software" constitutes all the programs people have developed to use the computer, such as spreadsheet, writing, presentations, photo handling, mail, and numerous other programs that make your hardware useful. And "application" is what we do with the device and its software, it is what yields results, new insights.

The apparent direct analogies are the human brain, the mind, and thoughts—i.e., what we choose to do with our brain and mind in our lives. The brain would be the biological aspect of that which enables our human species to experience life. It is located in a well-defined location within our body. The mind builds on the brain and can be trained. Education is the process of providing software for the mind. It ends up with "knowledge." And when we then properly employ knowledge to the tasks and opportunities that present themselves in our lives, we come to results that have meaning, which is the basis for consciousness. Hence, the trilogy hardware /software /application-results in the computer language translates to brain /knowledge / potential for consciousness.

The human brain provides, by a dimensionality, more than what a computer can do. It enables our senses to function, and it provides for the development of experiences like love and compassion, which are outside of the physical reality. The computer is characterized by complete objectivity and, therefore, reproducibility, while the brain functions in a subjective manner without inherent, guaranteed reproducibility of the results. A computer will produce a certain result when subjected to a set of directions – every time, with dependable certainty. It can learn, but only to the extent of programmed parameters. For example, the writing program of a computer can learn new words you may be using. Once you have used the new word, say, your somewhat unusual name, a few times, it will put it in its memory, and when you then start writing that name again, it will, already after the first or second letter, come back with the correct spelling of the entire name as an option for you to use. The computer will, however, never create a new context for that learned new word. That's what your mind will have to decide. The mind, even with the exact same input parameters and after having gone through the same training, will produce results that are not necessarily predictable and reproducible but may be different under different circumstances. This is because the mind takes subjective factors into consideration.

The brain and computer hardware are totally localized. Physical damage to either compromises the other two categories. Software and mind are semi-localized. If properly programmed, software can be used in various hardware configurations, such as in various computers. Within certain limits of hardware composition and compatibility constraints, software functions even in different brands of computers. Similarly, by education and training, the mind of different people can be accessed and conditioned. Application is wide open to literally any user and topic, and the results of applications are entirely independent of the hardware with which they were achieved. Similarly, what we do with our mind, how we apply it, is entirely independent of how we originally obtained the education and training of our mind, and the results of applying this great divine gift of a mind are located entirely outside of the person who did the application.

It is nowadays possible to design an entire airplane with a computer. Materials composition, aero-thermodynamics, stability aspects, airworthiness, the behavior in flight, all this can be designed with computer programs; and once the design has been completed, you can smash the computer and the design will live on nonetheless. The result has become separate from that with which it was generated, the computer and the software.

The two analogues, the brain and the computer, are far apart in terms of what we might call importance or complexity. After all, the computer was invented and developed by the other, the brain. Let us say that they are apart by a "dimensionality." The result of successful application of computer software is the resolution of "third-dimensional" problems,[120] such as mathematical calculations, architectural drawings, writing a book, financial projections, design of an airplane, or a flight to Mars. In particular also medical research and application, such as the study of symptoms and treatment statistics, the research and development of medicines, medical equipment, and surgical tools and procedures, are all of "third-dimensional" nature. We can call this result of software application an increase in complexity.

Commensurate with the location of a physical computer, the result of applying it can be anywhere in the physical universe. It can be as far away as the Tesla car in the tip of the rocket sent into solar

---

[120] We distinguish between "third-dimensional" and "forth-dimensional" aspects, not to confuse with the physical connotation of three-dimensional space and four-dimensional space-time. Everything that is physical, i.e., everything that is subject to the laws of physics, is "third-dimensional." And everything that is categorized as nonphysical is called "fourth-dimensional." With this definition, crop circles and orb recordings are all third-dimensional, because they are clearly physical manifestations, but that which originated them is forth-dimensional.

orbit by the engineers of SpaceX Corporation in February 2018. But it is still in the physical universe.

The result of certain rigorous applications of the mind is consciousness. Consciousness is not physical; it is a "forth-dimensional" quality. It is not confined to the 4-dimensional space-time physical reality. It is a "dimension" beyond that. It cannot be localized at all. It can not only be anywhere in space, or in the physical universe, but it can be anywhere, i.e., beyond any thing and beyond anything. It is beyond space and time. The rocket tip with the Tesla car will last for a very long time, most certainly surviving all of us, before it will—still being in the third-dimensional, physical reality and subject to its laws—eventually decay or disintegrate for one or the other physically explainable reason. However, consciousness, i.e., the product of the mind, generated by using a brain, will never decay or disappear, because it exists outside of space and time.

It is, in principle, physically possible to devise a mechanism with which one can retrieve and re-use a product obtained or devised with a computer. For example, if we were ever able to develop the proper space vehicle, and if we were to devote the time and effort and physical energy to design the project, we would, in principle, be able to retrieve that Tesla car before it disintegrates. It is, of course, unlikely that you and I will witness such a physical achievement in our lifetimes, but it is not impossible.

Similarly, it is possible to develop a means to retrieve consciousness from the "Field of Cosmic Consciousness." And herein lies the end of the analogy between the computer and the brain: while the mechanism for retrieval of the Tesla car is possible but not yet available to humankind, the "vehicle" to retrieve consciousness is here and now and in use all the time, without us being fully aware of this being so. We said that consciousness, once generated, is independent of space and time, which implies that it is also with us and around us all the time. The "vehicle" to retrieve it is like an antenna. Every person has such an antenna—some perhaps a bit better developed than others, and some are aware of its existence more than others. But we all have it.

This antenna is a fourth-dimensional "instrument." It is readily available to evolved beings in the nonphysical—or spiritual—reality; and it is, as we have hypothesized in the chapter on spiritual healing, extensively used for spirit-directed healing.

We summarize: the computer will never be a producer of consciousness in and by itself. It will only learn what we program into it. It will always remain a tool with which we, the human species, may enhance, or speed up, evolution and, hence, enhance the purpose of the **Grand Original Design**.

Let us now address the important subject of consciousness itself. What is it? How do we define it? People have different ideas of what consciousness is. We start, as we have pointed out elsewhere in this book, at the etymology of the word itself. If comes from the Latin word "*con-scire*," which we translate as "knowing in context," "knowing within a greater framework."

Rather than continuing to philosophize over this word, we will simply list a few examples of what we understand when we use the word consciousness:

- **An epiphanic moment of consciousness**: An astronaut, when he saw the Earth from outer space, was reported as having been deeply touched when he realized that everything which any human being has ever experienced is all confined to the one small sphere he was looking at, a small colorful ball in the black sky, with no visible boundaries: We are one humanity, endowed with awesome possibilities!

- **Service above self**: This motto of Rotary International, when sincerely enacted, is an act of consciousness. Rotary has been the primary driving force for essentially eradicating polio from the face of the earth, with millions of dollars selflessly contributed toward this cause.

- **Empathy for the less fortunate**: Selflessly making time and money available to feed the homeless.

- **Anonymous gifting**: A woman taught a friend her special art of alternative healing. Rather than accepting money for payment, she suggested to the friend to prepare several sealed envelopes with modest amounts of money,[121] and hand them anonymously to individuals she perceived as needy.

- **Unexpected sharing of food**: A man and his wife afforded themselves a delicious take-out dinner. On their way home, looking forward to enjoying the food, they passed by a couple of less fortunate persons. Without rationalization, they lovingly handed the bag with their take-out meal to them.

- **Deciding for the nobler alternative**: A young psychotherapist, still in need of patients to make ends meet, recommended to a wealthy patient, when he noticed that she was in good health and no longer in need of his services, to discontinue her sessions and make it on her own, even though she was eager to continue as patient, and the therapist needed the income.

- **Loving unconditionally**: When a young couple was unable to conceive, they decided to adopt a young boy. Then they saw another, severely handicapped boy and adopted him as well. Then they conceived and had two healthy children of their own. They reared all four children with unconditional, equal love, devotion, and attention.

- **Spilled milk**: A grandmother hosted a festive dinner at her house, with the best china and fancy table decorations. A young guest accidentally spilled a glass of milk all over the

---

[121] This suggestion by our Brazilian friend Anna Sharp included to use amounts in the mystical completion number of "3", such as $3.33, $33.33 or alike. Wayne Dyer also recommended this sort of anonymous gift giving.

table. To preempt the child's embarrassment, the gracious host "accidentally" spilled her own glass of red wine over the table, just stating, "Oh, accidents happen!"

- **Admitting a mistake**: While maneuvering his car out of a tight parking spot, a man caused a minor dent in another vehicle. Nobody saw it, and the other vehicle was quite old and banged up. He affixed his name and phone number on the windshield of the damaged vehicle before he drove off.

- **Allowing Infinite Intelligence**: A famous scientist retired from his prestigious ivy-league university professorship to devote the remaining years of his life, and all his life savings, to the study of nonhuman intelligence, not minding the criticism he received from his former scientific colleagues for conducting "pseudo-research."

- **"Why," not "how"**: A renowned historian made the subtle shift in emphasis of his exciting work from asking "how" things were, to being preoccupied with "Why are we here? Why am I here, in this life, in this place, on this planet? What is the deeper meaning behind what happened then and what is happening now?"

- **Action against own interest**: A senator, up for re-election, placed conscience higher than party-line in a crucial vote, fully knowing that this would jeopardize his re-election chances.

- **Truthfulness**: An elected politician admitted to having made a mistake, rather than lying about it.

- **Random acts of kindness**:
News headlines such as:

• *Turkish Bride and Groom Spent Their Wedding Day Feeding 4000 Refugees*
• *Entire Neighborhood Secretly Learns Sign Language to Surprise Deaf Neighbor*

• *McDonald's Employee Helped Elderly Disabled Man with his Food*

There are, of course, endless numbers of examples of life situations all of us have encountered that can complement this list. Consciousness is not esoteric, it is not out of reach for the common person. We are all "producing" consciousness. That's who we are! And that's who we are meant to be.

A moment of consciousness is characterized by being unselfish, loving, caring, forgiving, admitting the truth, understanding, happy for the success or well-being of others, wise, or by numerous other similar characteristics of natural human kindness, when extended as a result of an altruistic, often spontaneous decision for a nobler alternative. A moment of contributed consciousness will often be perceived by others as an action against own interest.

Consciousness has nothing to do with mental output, or a high IQ, or academic degrees, but it has everything to do with living a joyful, meaningful and fulfilling life.

APPENDIX (C)

THE ORB/EVP EXPERIMENT

".... Hey, that is banned from here! ..."

We were sitting opposite to her in a circle of about 20 seminarians in the cozy lecture room of Casa de Luz.[122] She looked like the Queen of Mexico; all dressed in the colors of the rainbow, her lips tomato red, a stern face, a hairdo like my mother—it was obvious she was the leader of the seminar.

We had never seen her or heard of her, except that she was listed as the leader of the weekend seminar we had signed up for, and that her address listed in the one-page roster of seminar participants was just a stone's-throw away from the house we had rented in Palo Alto for what was intended to be a one-year NASA post-doctoral assignment.

It was a Friday afternoon in March of 1970, and the introductory meeting was about to start. My thoughts were revolving around the theme that the supposedly famous leader of this seminar was living in a modest house in our neighborhood. I had expected something more illustrious. Someone with more notoriety, not "just a neighbor."

There was a strange tension in the room. Everybody was looking at that woman. You could have heard a needle drop on the carpeted floor. She was sitting on a folding chair, just like the rest of us in the room, slowly looking from person to person in the circle, sweeping

---

[122] "Casa de Luz" was one of several small lodges of the Sequoia Seminar grounds in the Santa Cruz mountains of California where Emilia and Dr. Harry Rathbun conducted their consciousness raising seminars. It was one of the first modest structures they had built on this expansive forest property, almost entirely with volunteer labor. During the ensuing years, we spent many weekend and week-long retreats at Sequoia Seminar. The Casa de Luz lodge itself burned down a few years after our first seminar there and was never re-built. The remainder of Sequoia Seminar was further developed and is, to this day, operated as a retreat center.

back and forth, not saying a word, with a stern face. Then her scanning motion stopped when she was looking at me. Still somewhat "Germanized"—I was the only male in the round who was wearing pleated pants and a necktie, as would have been customary for such an occasion in our home country—she took an eternity of perhaps half a minute and mustered me up and down, and down and up, then looked me in the eyes, for another eternity of at least ten seconds, with frowns constantly changing on her forehead, and then she broke the silence with just three words,

"You are aloof."

Then another pause, perhaps a half minute or so, waiting for an answer. None was forthcoming—we had just been in the country for less than half a year, and that word had not yet found its way into my vocabulary. I had a hunch what it might mean, but did not feel like admitting that I was intimidated. After all, I was 28 years old, had a Ph.D. from a renowned university in Germany—I was still unaware that these letters stand for "Pile High and Deep"—and was doing scientific research at NASA. The world belonged to me.

But then reality set in.

This first encounter with Emilia did exactly what it was meant to be. It changed my life. It enhanced our relationship in our marriage and in our family. It re-oriented my priorities. It marked the beginning of a journey for both of us that never ended. We would spend many more week-end and week-long retreats at Sequoia Seminar, under the leadership of Emilia and Harry Rathbun, as well as of other members of the inner circle of the "work" they had started and called *Creative Initiative*. Their message was simple but relentless: "Be the change, 100%" (see *Being the Change*, by Klaus and Gundi Heinemann, 2013, for details about their teachings).

Emilia Lindeman was born on January 1st, 1906, into a wealthy family in Mexico. She was sent to California for her education. In

1928 she graduated from San Jose State College with a teaching credential. She met her future husband, the intellectual, somewhat reserved twelve years older law professor Dr. Harry J. Rathbun, at a Stanford University faculty event. They married in 1931 and had two children.

In the early 1930s, Emilia and Harry were introduced to the Canadian business man and theologian *Dr. Henry Burton Sharman*, who held scholarly seminars on the *Teachings of Jesus of Nazareth* in his wilderness retreat center in northern Canada. In 1934, the Rathbuns participated in a 4-week retreat with Sharman. Emilia's experience at this seminar was a major turning point in her life. She decided to devote her life one hundred percent to God and stayed with this resolve until the time of her passing, 70 years later. She started a relentless life-long effort to build a community of people committed to work on "establishing the Kingdom of God on Earth."

As bread winner of the Rathbun family, Harry continued his promising career as full-time Law professor at Stanford University but passed on opportunities for promotions that would take time away from supporting the educational work of his wife. He retired as soon as he could, to be able to pursue his and Emilia's work of love for humanity full time. In the 1960s Harry and Emilia founded an educational work that became known as *Creative Initiative Foundation* and *Sequoia Seminar* and branched in the 1970s and 1980s to a hugely influential grass-roots NGO movement, involving more than 1000 highly motivated people, under the name *Beyond War*, which became a major contributor to the fall of the Iron Curtain in 1989. No one knows the exact number, but the people who have experienced Emilia and Harry and their work numbered many thousands.

After Harry's death in 1987 at the age of 93, Emilia continued to give all her time and energy to the Work of the foundations she and Harry had founded. We continued to benefit from her wisdom in countless evening meetings in ad-hoc groups in her home in Palo

Alto, until literally two weeks prior to her passing in 2004. It took another nine years until we were ready to attempt to put in print the actual elements of their profound teachings. The book *Being the Change*[123] was published in 2013.

Shortly before her passing, at age 98, the question about the realness of a "life hereafter" came up in a conversation we had with Emilia, and she agreed that she would try to give us a sign from the other side, if possible.

In the ensuing years, we felt that several specific incidences we experienced were likely Emilia's action on this promise, but nothing was really earth-shaking, and we dismissed them as inconclusive. But then, in 2008, four years after her passing, the proceedings of the *Orb/EVP Experiment* unraveled. It would give us a profound answer to the important question about the relationship between the spiritual and physical realities. Read on for details.

A few weeks after the publication of our first book on orbs, *The Orb Project*, in 2007, I received—totally out of the blue—an e-mail from a person who humbly introduced himself as "Alec," stating he is a specialist in "EVP." He had heard about our orbs research activities and was wondering if I was interested in an experiment where we would try to correlate the appearance of orbs during EVP sessions.

I googled and found out that Alec MacRae[124] was a renowned expert in electronic voice phenomena (commonly known as EVP), a field I knew nothing about. The Internet revealed that EVP is a genuine physical phenomenon, measurable with highly sensitive sound recording instruments. It exhibits some of the characteristics

---

[123] *Being the Change – how one contemporary person initiated extraordinary change in the world by following the wisdom teachings with totality,* by Klaus and Gundi Heinemann, 2013.

[124] Proprietor of *Alexander MacRae Research.*

of normal speech, but coming from no physically verifiable origin.[125] There are quite a few scientists involved in EVP research, and Alec had a superb reputation among them.

It took almost a year, and numerous e-mail exchanges, until we were able to conduct the first, crude experiment. Gundi and I were keynote speakers at a conference on orbs in 2008 in Glastonbury, UK, and Alec, who lived in Scotland, was able to interrupt his return travel from an EVP symposium in Spain to meet with us in a hotel in Glastonbury.

We met in Alec's bland hotel room. He had brought his EVP equipment—essentially a small, sophisticated sound recorder—and we brought our camera. The objective was to "contact" a person in the other realm and to attempt to receive a message. For obvious reasons we selected Emilia Rathbun who was entirely unknown to Alec, and we made sure to disclose nothing about her to him. All he knew was that we were contacting with our minds "a person whom we knew well and who had deceased several years ago."

After a few minutes of getting acquainted, we got down to the objective of the meeting. Alec set up his recorder, which looked very much like a small audio tape-recorder. On his signal he started recording, and we silently invoked the presence of the spirit of Emilia, asking her to give us a sign from where she was, if possible. Meanwhile, one of us took photos of the white hotel room opposite to where we were seated, to see if any orbs showed up. After about three minutes, Alec announced that the experiment was completed. He remarked that it would take him about two weeks to analyze the recording, and he would then get back to us via email with the results.

We also agreed that, if there was any sign of success, we would devise a more elaborate program, where we would be at different

---

[125] Actually, EVP recordings usually come in short, fast voice-like "utterings" of typically just a few words that are often difficult to decipher. It is, therefore, customary in EVP expert circles to solicit corroboration of the interpretation of EVP utterings by other EVP specialists.

locations, Alec in his laboratory in Scotland and we back home in California. At a precise, prearranged synchronized time, we would then again invoke this diseased person's spirit presence and ask very specific identifying questions. The spirit's (i.e., Emilia's) name, her gender, and the actual questions would be kept secret until after Alec had analyzed the answers. We were hoping that this experiment, if designed skeptic-proof, could, once and for all, prove that there is life after death.

About a couple of weeks after the Glastonbury experiment, we received an email from Alec. He prefaced his results with the remark that he figured the experiment had produced nothing to speak of, except for a four-word uttering which he identified as "Hallelujah - High Street - Band," but which did not make any sense to him.

Little did he know that this uttering did make a lot of sense to us! "High Street" was the name of the street where of Emilia and Harry's Foundation office[126] was located. Many meetings took place at "High Street;" it was clearly a name that was in very frequent use by several hundreds of people who were active in the *Creative Initiative* and, later, *Beyond War* organizations. Over a period of several years, Gundi and I would go to meetings at High Street probably at least twice a week. "Hallelujah" was a favorite expression of enthusiastic response of Emilia. And "Band," we figured, could easily have been a slight sound misinterpretation by Alec of the first name of our philosopher-friend, Ben Young, with whom I had spent numerous discussion meetings in the late 1990s, and who also knew Emilia well but was, of course, also entirely unknown to Alec.

The orb photography part of this experiment did not work out too well. With its bright white walls, the hotel room was not suited for orb photography, and we saw only a few, faint orbs, but we were nevertheless elated about these results.

---

[126] The offices of *Creative Initiative Foundation, Sequoia Seminar, Beyond War,* and *Foundation for Global Community*, the charitable organizations founded by Emilia Rathbun and her husband Harry Rathbun were, for several decades, located at 222 High Street in Palo Alto, California.

We did not divulge any of the specifics of our interpretation to Alec, but did let him know that these results did make sense to us and we were very much encouraged to proceed to the next stage of the project. We then went ahead with the planning for the detailed follow-up experiments, where Emilia was supposed to prove her identity in the other realm.

We prepared a set of very specific questions for her to respond to, which only she would be able to answer correctly, while Alec would not have a clue about which Spirit Entity we were planning to invoke, nor about the nature of the questions we would ask. We kept the questions securely locked in the office of a notary public, to be released only after the completion of the experiment and Alec's neutral evaluation. We figured that, if Alec would come back with utterings indicating correct answers to the questions for which he knew no context, this would be proof that Emilia is present in the nonphysical reality.

The timing was arranged with utmost care, such that Alec's recording took place exactly during the three minutes of our concentration on Emilia with these specific questions, and the timing of the utterings, if any, identified in the recordings could be correlated with the timing when the questions were asked. The experiment was to be repeated twice, at the same time on consecutive days.

The 3-stage experiment took place two months later, in late December of 2008. Everything seemed to go as planned. Even the pictures taken in Alex' laboratory show orbs,[127] whereby a relation of these orbs to Emilia can, of course, not conclusively be confirmed.

---

[127] It was remarkable that these photos showed several orbs at all. They were taken without flash and at relative long exposure times to compensate for the low lighting conditions in Alec's laboratory, i.e., under conditions that would normally not be conducive for orb photography. Going by what we now know about orb photography, we can state that the Entity in the nonphysical realm that emanated these orbs did its best to produce orbs in the photos even under adverse photographic conditions.

Again, Alec prefaced his e-mail, which we received about two weeks later, with a remark that he was disappointed about the uttering he analyzed from the first of the three recordings. But then, so were we when we first heard it. Rather than the expected concrete answers to our questions, the voice recording received by Alec contained only one distinct uttering:

"Hey, that is banned from here."

That said it all—for us! While Alec was, understandably, disappointed that no "interesting" answers had come through—except for this one short phrase which he figured had no relation to the experiment—the answer was, from our perspective, even though not anticipated, entirely authentic, plausible, and complete. It made all the sense in the world! It told us that the degree of authenticity and assurance we had hoped to yield from the experiment was not going to be forthcoming. It stated that it transgressed the delineation between the spiritual and physical realities.[128]

This conclusion confirms very generally the law of increasing consciousness which we have discussed at various stages of this book. If we were able to receive unequivocally—and the emphasis is on this word, unequivocally, without a sliver of a doubt—messages from the unseen reality, such that even hard-nosed critics would have to admit that they are irrefutable, which is what we were naively going for, then the actual purpose of our existence would be compromised. We are here for our essence to grow in consciousness. The basis for growing in consciousness, which is love manifested by altruistic decisions for the good, is removed when we receive directions that indicate without any doubt which decisions are the right ones for us to take. Such decisions are then not be based on a real choice. Only when a real choice is involved, a decision becomes "a resolve of a

---

[128] Given that analyses of EVP recordings are very time consuming and, therefore, expensive, we then refrained from further analysis of the recordings taken on days two and three of the experiment, because the answer we had obtained was, from our perspective, entirely authentic and complete.

nobler alternative," as Harry and Emilia used to phrase it, and only then does it bear the potential to increase consciousness.

From where she was, Emilia[129] had given us exactly the answer we needed to hear, which is that no matter how much we would strive for certainty about the life hereafter, we will not get such a certainty.

The mystery remains. It must remain. We are given signs and hints and lots of active help from the other side, but they will be communicated as phenomena, not facts. We have the birth right to grow in consciousness. Consciousness is based on a choice of the nobler alternative. This is part of the Plan, part of the **Grand Original Design**.

---

[129] We actually have no way of knowing who or what it was that gave us the uttering. It could have been Emelia's spirit, or some other "phenomenal" nonphysical entity responding on her behalf. In fact, it was not customary for Emilia to start any message or address with the word "Hey." But the profundity of the answer we received, "Hey, that is banned from here," under the circumstances, is independent of this uncertainty.

APPENDIX (D)

RECOMMENDATIONS FOR ORB PHOTOGRAPHY

During the years since we first published about orb photography (in 2007), the optical qualities of smart phones have been significantly improved, and more and more people revert to their cell phone for all their photography; and people keep wondering why they don't see as many orbs in their photos as they used to. We therefore want to remind our readers in this chapter in the Appendix what they should look out for to obtain high-resolution orb photos.

For best orb photography consider the following:

■ **Ask**: It is recommended to approach orb photography with a certain degree of reverence toward the Entities on the other side of the reality veil who originate them. Understand that you are not photographing "objects," that you are not trying to "catch" or "hunt for" orbs, but that genuine orbs are appearing on your photo recordings by non-human intent. They are generated by highly evolved non-human intelligence, generally for a specific purpose.

■ **Use a point-and-shoot camera with "CCD" charge plate and high-intensity flash**: Best for orb photography are dedicated "point and shoot" cameras, designed for single-frame photography, in the low to mid (US$100-200) price range. The single most important requirement is that your camera should have a "CCD" sensor, which is better suited for single-photon sensitivity than the "CMOS" sensors that are now more commonly used in cameras, because they are a bit less expensive.[130] Point and shoot cameras will typically

---

[130] The sensor type is usually mentioned in the technical specifications section of the camera description. If you cannot find that particular CCD specification, assume that a CMOS sensor is used and move on to the next available product. I found a good description of the significant differences for single-photon detection between DDC and CMOS sensors at https://electronics.howstuffworks.com/cameras-photography/digital/question362.htm.

have a high-intensity flash that would allow outside flash photography reaching well into the 15-30 feet distance range.

- **Do not use a smart phone**: Smart phones have only very low-intensity flash capability (intended for close-up photography), and it is typically cumbersome to engage that flash on a smart phone. Also, the lens and charge plate geometries of smart phones are not congenial for orb photography. We do see orbs with smart phones, but they are very limited in resolution.

- **Do not use a movie camera in the still photo mode**: It is tempting to employ a good movie camera, such as a *Sony Handycam*, in the still photo mode. While higher-priced Handycam cameras are excellent in both modes, they do have a CMOS sensor and do not normally have an efficient and/or easy-to-engage single-photo flash capability, which renders them impractical for orb photography.

- **Engage the flash**: Make it a habit to always engage the flash when you use your point-and-shoot camera and hope to record orbs. If you see "orbs" in photos taken without flash, they are very likely lens reflections from bright objects in the field of view. For even better orb photography use an external flash, i.e., one that is not built into the camera but mounted on top of it with a "hot shoe" attachment. Even low-cost external flashes ($30-100 price range) can be directed such that they can be pointed upward rather than in the direction of the photographed scene.[131] This will provide more indirect lighting energy for the orb generation process, and the interiorities of the orbs may show higher contrast.

- **Shoot not just one but many photos**: Storage media for digital photography are cheap. Do not hesitate to shoot many photos or photo series. However, do remember that the flash

---

[131] This recommendation applies only when you are photographing inside a room. For outside photography, your flash should be directed at your field of view.

requires electronic re-charging, which may take a few seconds between taking photos.

- **Take at least two or three photos of each scene**: This very important recommendation will enable you to discern if an orb is genuine. If the orb shows only in one of the photos, and at a different location or not at all in another photo, it is very likely genuine. If you see an orb-like figure in approximately the same location in two or more shots taken from the same scene, it is almost certainly not a genuine orb but likely a lens reflection from a light source in front of the camera, or a camera defect.

- **Shoot against a dark background**: Orbs are low-intensity, slightly opaque features that are much easier discernable against a dark than a bright background. Taking photos in a darkened room is ideal for orbs from highly evolved beings; photographing outside against the night sky may yield, additionally, also orb-like "nature spirits" which are pretty but, due to their large numbers in any one photo, less prone to conveying and/or understanding messages.

- **Fewer is better than many**: This recommendation is counter-intuitive. People are often elated when they see many orbs in a photo. If you have only one distinct orb in your photo, your chances of understanding a message it might present to you are best.

- **Avoid scenes with point lights**: Light sources in front of the camera, such as the sun or street lanterns or single light bulbs, *even if not directly in the field of view*, will easily cause lens reflections.

- **Avoid dust, fog, mist, rain or snow**: Images of such "suspended particles," if they are within about 2-5" from your camera lens, will look very similar to genuine orbs and are often indistinguishable from them. Therefore, it is strongly advisable not to attempt to take orb photos under such environmental conditions.

REFERENCES

PRINTED MEDIA

- Brown, Sylvia, "Phenomenon – Everything you need to know about the Paranormal," *Penguin Group*, 2006.
- Dyer, Wayne, "Wishes Fulfilled," *Hay House Inc*, 2017.
- Greer, Stephen "Disclosure: Military and Government Witnesses Reveal the Greatest Secrets in Modern History," 2001.
- Heinemann, Klaus "Consciousness or Entropy? A Guide Toward a Fresh Understanding of Man's Purpose & Required Response," *ISBN 0-9630502-0-6*, 1991.
- Heinemann, Klaus and Gundi, "Orbs – Their Mission and Messages of Hope," *Hay House Inc*, 2010.
- Heinemann, Klaus with Heinemann, Gundi, "Expanding Perception – Re-Discovering the Grand Original Design," *ISBN 978-1492910800*, 2013.
- Heinemann, Klaus and Gundi, "Being the Change – how one contemporary person initiated extraordinary change in the world by following the wisdom teachings with totality," *ISBN 978-1493673643*, 2013.
- Hernandez, Rey, Klimo, Jon and Schild, Rudy, "Beyond UFOs: The Science of Consciousness and Contact with Non-Human Intelligence," *FREE Foundation*, 2018.
- Laurentin, Rene, and Joyeux, Henri, "Scientific and Medical Studies on the Apparitions at Medjugorje," *Veritas Publications*, 1986; First English Language Edition (December 31, 1987).
- Ledwith, Miceal, and Heinemann, Klaus, "The Orb Project," *Atria Books – Beyond Words Publishing*, 2007
- Tiller, William A., "Psycho-Energetic Science," *Pavior Publ.* 2007.

- Vos, Ed, "Orbs en andere lichtfenomenen: multidimensionale bewustzijnsvormen," *AnkhHermes, Uitgeverij*, 2009.
- Xavier, Francisco C., "Nosso Lar – A Spiritual Home," originally published in Portuguese in 1943, publ. in English by the *Allan Kardec Educational Society*, 2000.

WEB LINKS

- *Aamc.org.* "Total Graduates by U.S. Medical School and Sex, 2013-2014 through 2017-2018, Tb. B-2.2." Accessed September 26, 2019. https://www.aamc.org/system/files/reports/1/factstableb2-2.pdf.

- *Azquotes.com.* Accessed September 24, 2019. https://www.azquotes.com/quote/1404030.

- *Cropcircleconnector.com*, updated July 23, 2019. Accessed 24 September 2019. http://www.cropcircleconnector.com/anasazi/cons96.html.

- "Drake Equation: Estimating the Odds of Finding E.T." By Elizabeth Howell, April 06, 2018. *Space.com.* Accessed September 24, 2019. https://www.space.com/25219-drake-equation.html.

- Heinemann Gundi, "Author Bio." *HealingGuidance.net.* Accessed 24 September 2019. https://www.healingguidance.net/gundi.

- Heinemann Gundi, "Paintings by Gundi Heinemann." *HealingGuidance.net.* Accessed September 24, 2019. https://www.healingguidance.net/paintings-by-gundi-heinemann/

- Heinemann, Klaus. "Author Bio." *HealingGuidance.net.* Accessed 24 September 2019. https://www.healingguidance.net/klaus/.

- Heinemann, Klaus & Gundi. "Books." *HealingGuidance.net.* Accessed 24 September 2019. https://www.healingguidance.net/books/.

- Heinemann, Klaus & Gundi. "Magnificence." *HealingGuidance.net.* Accessed 26 September 2019. http://www.healingguidance.net/magnificence/.

- Heinemann, Klaus & Gundi. "Moving Orbs." *TheHeinemanns.net.* Accessed September 24, 2019. https://www.theheinemanns.net/Moving-Orbs.mp4.

- Heinemann, Klaus & Gundi. "Orbs." *HealingGuidance.net.* Accessed on 24 September 2019. https://www.healingguidance.net/orbs.

- Heinemann, Klaus & Gundi. "Phenomena." *HealingGuidance. net*. Accessed 24 September 2019. https://www.healingguidance. net/phenomena.
- Heinemann, Klaus. "The orb phenomenon: bridging to the world beyond?" *Light, Vol 134, No 1, Spring 2013*. Accessed September 24, 2019. https://www.theheinemanns.net/Light5-13.pdf.
- Heinemann, Klaus & Gundi. "The Orb Project." *The Heinemanns. net*. Accessed September 24, 2019. https://www.theheinemanns. net/orbproject.htm.
- *How Stuff Works*. "What is the difference between CCD and CMOS image sensors in a digital camera?" Accessed September 27, 2019. https://electronics.howstuffworks.com/cameras-photography/digital/question362.htm.
- *IMDb*. "Vitus (2006)." Accessed September 24, 2019. https://www.imdb.com/title/tt0478829/.
- *Out of Body Experience Research Foundation OBERF*. Accessed September 24, 2019. https://www.oberf.org/
- Sheldrake, Rupert. "The Crop Circle Making Competition." *Sheldrake.org*. Accessed September 24, 2019. https://www.sheldrake.org/essays/the-crop-circle-making-competition.
- *Wikipedia, the free encyclopedia*. "Catholic Church response to the Medjugorje apparitions." Accessed 24 September 2019. https://en.wikipedia.org/wiki/Catholic_Church_response_to_the_Medjugorje_apparitions.
- *Wikipedia, the free encyclopedia*. "Cleve Backster." Accessed September 24, 2019. https://en.wikipedia.org/wiki/Cleve_Backster.
- *Wikipedia, the free encyclopedia*. "Fermi Paradox." Accessed September 24, 2019. https://en.wikipedia.org/wiki/Fermi_paradox.
- *Wikipedia, the free encyclopedia*. "Hypothetical Types of Biochemistry." Accessed September 26, 2019. https://en.wikipedia.org/wiki/Hypothetical_types_of_biochemistry.
- *Wikipedia, the free encyclopedia*. "International Association for Near-Death Studies." Accessed September 24, 2019. https://

en.wikipedia.org/wiki/International_Association_for_Near-Death_Studies.

- *Wikipedia, the free encyclopedia.* "Our Lady of Fátima." Accessed September 24, 2019. https://en.wikipedia.org/wiki/Our_Lady_of_Fátima.
- *Your Dictionary.com.* Accessed September 24, 2019. https://www.yourdictionary.com/time#s1morazPkRX0lJvU.99.

Printed in the United States
By Bookmasters